KEW

b

David Blomfield and Christopher May

The Richmond Local History Society
2009

ISBN 978-0-9550717-4-4

Printed in Great Britain by Doppler Press, 5 Wates Way,
Brentwood, Essex CM15 9TB

Contents

Front cover illustration: Beechwood Avenue in 1940
(Photo courtesy Richmond Local Studies Collection)
Back cover illustration: Aerial photo of the camp occupied by the
American troops and Italian POWs

Preface

Much of the material in this book will remind some readers of their own wartime experiences, for Kew's wartime memories are in many ways similar to those of other British villages: they too housed evacuees, collected bomb debris, ran from doodlebugs. However, Kew's wartime story includes a special factor, as it was for three years host to a base camp used first by American soldiers and then by Italian POWs, with inevitable complications for the residents' own lives.

We owe a debt to the Kew Society and the National Archives for the efforts they have made to commemorate 'Kew Barracks', as the camp was called by the GIs. The Archives attracts visitors from all over the world, and it is right that the information board now erected in front of the building should remind them of the international impact of that World War. The camp is the subject of two separate chapters in this book, and some of the text and pictures come from two unique 'Souvenir Books' created by the American soldiers. It is, however, equally important that we commemorate the impact of the war on everyday life in the village itself, and thIS is the subject matter of the other chapters, most of them heavily dependent on contributions from those who lived through the war in Kew.

We are grateful to Jim Mitchell, Rod Emmerson and Isabel Wilson for their research. and to all those who have allowed us to include their reminiscences in this book. Some of these were gathered in 2005 by Ian Hunter for his *Personal Memories of life in Kew in the first half of the 20th Century* (Richmond Local History Society). Others were gathered by Pat Thomas to complement her photographs in her *Kew through my Camera Lens*, and by the Museum of Richmond for their 1993 exhibition, Richmond at War. Further reminiscences were contributed later at meetings hosted by Kew Library and the Kew Avenue Club in 2009. We hope these contributions will inspire others to suggest amendments and additions to future editions of this book. Local history does not stand still; it welcomes new material. So, as the book's editors, we say to all our readers: 'Do please get in touch with us, bring us your mementos, tell us your stories.' We want the second edition of this book to be bigger and better, but that will depend on you.

David Blomfield , 7 Leyborne Park, Kew, TW9 3HB 020 8940 8749
Christopher May, 87 Ennerdale Road, Kew, TW9 2DN 020 8948 8338

CHAPTER 1 – *Introduction*

This book aims to recapture the flavour of life in Kew in the Second World War, using wherever possible the recollections of those who lived here at that time. However, let us first set those recollections in context. Kew had experienced war many times before – first in the days when it was scarcely a hamlet, then when it was an independent village and lastly in its early years as one of London's dormitory suburbs.

There is a possibility that when Julius Caesar fought his way across the Thames in 54 BC he did so at the Great Ford that could then be crossed on foot downstream of what is now Syon House. More certainly in 1016 the Danes under Canute and the Saxons under Edmund Ironside fought a series of battles on both sides of the ford. The fighting proved futile. The Saxons won the battles, only to lose the war: before the year was out, Edmund was dead and the field left clear for Canute. For Kew too nothing changed. If one of the battles was fought, as seems likely, right across what is now the Royal Botanic Gardens, the contestants – or more likely the camp followers – did an excellent job in tidying up after the event. No signs of the fighting remain.

In subsequent conflicts, such as the Wars of the Roses and the Civil War, Kew seems to have been spared major battles, but in the nineteenth century it was affected, as was every village, by the Napoleonic Wars. Each county then had to contribute men to the war effort, or be fined for the shortfall. In March 1805 Surrey was short on its contribution by 1010 men, and the fine of £20,200 was divided amongst its parishes, Kew having to pay £22-18-4. Meanwhile, at an historic meeting in St Anne's in 1803, Kew pledged to raise what was the equivalent of a Home Guard force. This force trained on Kew Green, as did other soldiers. At the end of the Napoleonic wars, the wall of Kew Gardens was decorated by a mural of over 800 ships, each of them five or six feet long. The mural was presumably accepted as a patriotic tribute to the navy, as the sailor who had painted the ships waited confidently beside his handiwork to be rewarded for his initiative rather than being clapped into the lock-up for graffiti.

Lastly – and within only a few years of the outbreak of the Second World War – Kew lost many men in what was called the Great War: a garden in Westerly Ware is dedicated to their memory, and their names are listed at St Anne's and St Luke's. Among them was a VC, Captain William Johnston RE, awarded the medal in the year before he was killed.

It was not, however, just men that Kew sent to war. They sent aeroplanes as well. On the riverside, the Glendower Aircraft Company established the first sizable industrial operation in Kew, a factory which built initially De Haviland DH4 light biplane bombers, and then Salamanders. Virginia Woolf recorded in her diaries that a Zeppelin dropped a bomb on Kew. In fact, it fell north of the bridge, but the Germans might have been aiming at the Kew factory.

All villages, of course, have similar memories and memorials. Yet Kew had something extra to commemorate. During the war it became a mecca for ministers, bishops, prime ministers, and innumerable members of the royal family. They came not to visit the Gardens, nor any of the elegant houses round the Green, but what is now and was even then the least prepossessing building in the whole of Kew—the former Victoria Working Men's Club, on the east side of Sandycombe Road.

This building has an unusual history. It stood originally on the site of St Luke's House. Built mostly of corrugated iron, it was from 1876 to 1889 an 'iron church' that housed both St Luke's church and St Luke's school. When the new church was built in the Avenue, the iron building was moved across the road to make room for the new school buildings. In 1892 it was opened as a social club. In the Great War, a member who had been employed as a builder at Buckingham Palace apparently persuaded the Prince of Wales to attend the club's annual dinner, and the Prince in turn persuaded his parents to visit it too. The club then became famous for the amount of money it raised to send cigarettes to men at the front, and it was presumably this that attracted visits from some fifty VIPs over seven years—probably a unique record for a club of its size, and most certainly for one set in such accommodation.

Although Kew's role in most of these earlier wars was long forgotten by 1939, it was not entirely irrelevant to its experiences in the Second World War. The earliest of these clashes were the inevitable outcome of Kew's unique positioning at the lowest point at which the Thames could at one time regularly be crossed on foot. The later ones were common to most villages in the south east, especially those close to London and vulnerable to the first wave of any successful invasion. As will be seen in Chapter 2, Kew's position on the river and its close relationship to the capital were again to be major factors in its fortunes in the Second World War.

CHAPTER 2 – *Blitz!*

For those living in and around London, the war really began with the start of the Blitz in September 1940. It was then that they suddenly found themselves in the front line, with their families and homes in constant danger of destruction. Yet both the official records and personal diaries remind us that the story began far earlier, in 1938-9.

We tend to look back with some contempt at the government of that time, because it failed to stop Hitler in his tracks. It is easy to forget that it devoted this period of uneasy peace to an extraordinarily thorough campaign that prepared the country for war. There were floods of leaflets that advised householders on what food to store, on anti-aircraft precautions, on the availability of shelters. The impact of these leaflets is briefly covered in the next chapter. Here it is necessary simply to remind ourselves that when the war broke out in September 1939 the whole country had been told what to expect.

With so much information from the government, and with the First World War fresh in the memory, everyone knew that the men would have go out to fight and that, judging from the course of the Spanish Civil War, their families would have to cope with horrific bombing of their homes. So there was no surprise that, on the outbreak, the government immediately evacuated half the children from London to the countryside. They were followed by several families from suburbs such as Kew, who made their own arrangements. Yet the war began with an unexpected lull. Conscription had begun in April to boost the numbers in the services, and the army moved across the Channel to aid our allies in France and the Low Countries, but there was no bombing of British cities until France fell, and before then there was the humiliating, and yet heroic, withdrawal from Dunkirk. It was the passing of the armada of little boats from the upper tidal Thames going to the rescue at Dunkirk that gave Kew residents the first reminder that this war was largely to be played at home.

'It was absolutely amazing,' Judy Strange recalled, 'this chug, chug, chug, all the way down the river. All these little boats – anything people could get hold of – went down the river to the sea across to France to rescue people from Dunkirk. I remember it vividly; it was like walking on a knife edge. We could hear it all going on in the tennis club.'

Perhaps that was what we might now call a wake-up call. For Judy Strange's tennis club (Priory Park), and for all the comfortable middle-class amenities of Kew, the world was about to change. The troops were rescued from Dunkirk in May and June 1940. The long awaited Blitz began in September 1940.

The first raid on Kew was on 9 September at 3.55 am. Eight HE (High Explosive) bombs fell in a line, hitting houses in the roads that lay between Sandycombe Road and Kew Road. Lichfield, Ennerdale, Clarence, Victoria Cottages, Lawn Crescent, The Avenue, Alexandra, and Gordon were all hit. That first raid was not only shocking in its intensity but also one of the most destructive of all the raids on Kew. It is not always possible to equate the ARP 'Bomb Reports' with the list of 'Bombed Sites' (see pages 66-71) but it is clear that this raid not only hit nos. 8-11 Clarence Rd and nos. 23-7 Alexandra; it totally destroyed them.

This pattern was typical of the kind of bombing the village was to endure for the next six months. The general assumption at the time and subsequently has been that Kew was not so much targeted by the Germans as used as a dumping ground for spare bomb loads. It seems likely that the German crews were instructed to concentrate their attack on London itself, and then follow the line of the river to the bend at Kew Bridge before turning for home. If they had failed to release all their bombs by then, they were ordered to drop them on residential areas. The earlier they dropped them, the lighter their loads and the swifter their journey home; so they dropped them on Kew.

However, it may be possible that the Germans had a further motive for dropping bombs on Kew. After that first burst of bombing alongside Sandycombe Road, most of the HE bombs dropped on Kew during the Blitz dropped close to the Chrysler works (now Kew Retail Park), five of them in one raid on 8 March 1941. The Germans may have known that aircraft were being built there, as they had been in the First World War. (The work at the factory is briefly reviewed in Chapter 3.)

Whatever the reason for this bombardment, from September 1940 to March 1941 there were to be air-raid warnings almost every night, and 19 raids in which bombs were dropped specifically on Kew. According to the records kept by the ARP, the following bombs were dropped on Kew: 66 High Explosive, 3 Oil, 3 Land Mines and innumerable incendiaries dropped on at least 48 sites.

Of all these bombs the most terrible were the 'Land Mines'. They contained huge quantities of explosive and floated down on parachutes. It was, for instance, a land mine that totally destroyed the whole of Peldon Avenue, in Richmond, on 20 September 1940, the worst loss in the borough, and similar destruction could have befallen the south end of Sandycombe Road on 26 September. The terse ARP listing simply records a 'mine' at 139 Sandycombe Road. What it does not record is that this land mine never landed. Its parachute became entangled on the roof of no. 139. Some residents remember that the authorities could supply no professional bomb disposal unit; so two local handymen – their names no longer known – defused the bomb on their own. Other residents maintain that the work was done by professionals. Whoever they were, happily they succeeded and were rewarded with a whip-round organised by their neighbours, who seem to have hung around to watch, completely confident of their expertise!

The land mine defused. Sandycombe Road says thanks.

Kew residents who lived through those months of bombardment admit to being frightened by the raids – and with good reason – but they do not seem to be have lost their nerve. They even recall those days with a certain macabre relish.

The most important factor in their lives was the location of the nearest air-raid shelter. The choice was surprisingly wide. By 1940 many households had their own Anderson shelters in their gardens. These shelters were constructed of steel and had been made available by local authorities since 1938. They were supplied free to families with income below £250. Others had to pay.

Roy Featherstone recalls that his family's Anderson shelter was, like many of them, 'sunk into the ground. There were bunks for my sister and me. Mum and Dad slept on the floor.' However, 'most people didn't like sleeping outside because it was damp and spooky.' Subsequently the Featherstones acquired a Morrison Shelter, which fitted inside the house. 'It was like a large table with steel uprights, steel top and bottom. It became our dining room table.' Morrisons rapidly became popular and were especially useful for those households that had no garden space.

An Anderson Shelter in Temple Road (Photo Pat Thomas)

Many families, however – even those that had shelters – preferred to sleep under the stairs or in cellars. Pat Thomas recalls: 'We slept on bunks in the cellar under my father's chemist shop in Mortlake Terrace. Several neighbours shared this dark "bedroom" with us, as did some enormous spiders!'

Elsewhere in Kew, sharing was the norm. Winifred Fortune of West Park Avenue recalled that 'in the Blitz we could read by the glare', and that when the siren went she and her husband would go all the way to Station Avenue to take refuge in the cellars under Robbins the ironmongers.

There were also a number of shelters accessible in the streets throughout the village. There is no official record of where they were sited, but there were large ones in Defoe Avenue and the back of Forest Road, and an even larger one in North Sheen Rec. Still more secure, if less inviting, was a honeycomb of shelters dug deep below the 'Little Green', one entrance being at the end of Gloucester Road. The schools had their own shelters, two by the pond for the King's School and one in Sandycombe Road for St Luke's.

Entrance to the Kew Green shelters
(Photo courtesy Richmond Local Studies Collection)

During the Blitz, life became a kaleidoscope of triumph and terror. 'The sky was full of barrage balloons at one stage,' Pat Thomas recalls. 'At night we'd go out and look at them and we'd hear the bombers coming over. Suddenly the searchlights would converge in a circle on a German plane. My mother would get excited and say: "Look, they have found one!" The artillery would start and they'd blast them out of the sky. They would explode and we'd all cheer. Then the next moment we would be down in the shelter hearing the bombs exploding and all the windows breaking. I remember lying there listening, and how your heart stopped beating at the screaming of the high explosive bombs.'

Local authority during the air raids was largely in the hands of the ARP, who established a regime that was on the whole unquestioned by their fellow residents. If they said that your blackout was inadequate, you got to work to set it right. If they said you must get off the streets, you got off double quick. Many of them were old soldiers from the previous war, and this, of course, added to their authority. They might be judged too old to fight again, but they were used to taking decisions. They now made their contribution in the ARP, in the Home Guard (which had a unit in Richmond) or as fire watchers.

Judy Strange has given this description of her father's role: 'Father was hardly ever in at night. He was in his ARP hut on the Green. He went round to call on people – women left alone with their children – he would knock on their doors and see if they were alright. He was like a kind of social worker, helping with all kind of problems, filling in forms and so on. Those old soldiers did so much good work.'

Those who were children at the time were equally in awe of the ARP's authority. The issue here was that the children were absorbed with building up collections of shrapnel and bomb debris. Generally this would do no more than burn their fingers, but when they starting collecting live bombs the wardens read the riot act. 'One day the Green was covered with unexploded incendiaries,' Pat Thomas recalls. 'They still had their webbing straps attached; so several of us grabbed two apiece and marched up to Mr Kimber to ask him what to do with them. He went white and said through gritted teeth: "Just put them down – very, very gently."'

To get some impression of the impact of this bombardment on Kew, we have to analyse the statistics on the loss of buildings and the loss of life. The record of 'Bombed Sites' (see pages 66-69) shows that Kew certainly lost at least 34 houses from the Blitz. This has to be treated as the minimum, as there are memories and indications that some roads may have lost more, and Kew would also lose a further 8 houses, after the Blitz, in West Park Avenue from the V2 in 1944. Compared with what the East End or Coventry suffered this was nothing, but it was still a shocking loss for a village as small as Kew. To this has to be added the frightening and frequent experience of having your windows blown out (despite liberal use of sticky tape) and your tiles rearranged by the blast of bombs. Bombs in Strand on the Green, for instance, regularly blew out windows round the Green.

As for loss of life, we know only that the official records show that 26 civilians died as a result of bombing in Kew, 19 of them during the Blitz. Each of these deaths must have been a shocking loss for the community – families of soldiers are conscious every minute of the day of the risks they run, but civilian deaths in war are harder to accept – yet it is extraordinary that with so much destruction there was so little loss of life in Kew. Credit must given to the shelters, to the ARP, and ultimately to the commonsense of the families who took what precautions they could. They seem to have been remarkably effective.

The Mini Blitz

In April 1941, the terrible months of the Blitz came to an end. The nightly terror eased. The sirens ceased to wail. The Luftwaffe had not been beaten, but they had certainly been beaten off. The Germans would continue throughout the war to pick targets and pulverise them as best they could, but they no longer mounted blanket raids on the south-east of England. Richmond and Kew were left in peace for almost three years, apart from one raid late at night in November 1943 which destroyed the Russell School in Petersham, fortunately with no loss of life

Yet, as can be seen from the ARP records on pages 66-71, there was to be a brief resumption of bombing raids early in 1944. These raids naturally raised fears that the Blitz was to be resumed, but Kew and Richmond were hit on only three nights. For one teenager, Ron Draper, for his family and for the Boathouse pub (just upstream of Kew Bridge), one of these raids was especially memorable.

'February 24th 1944 was my mother's fortieth birthday. As this was only a week or so after my grandmother's birthday the family had arranged to meet at the Boathouse for a quiet drink. Despite a sudden spate of short sharp air-raids (the first for over two years) it was decided that the arrangements should stand.

'This suited me as my uncle was a friend of the publican and on these rare occasions I was allowed to sit in the hotel's kitchen. Added to this was the prospect of a fizzy grapefruit drink and if available a bag of Smith's crisps.

'I had already arranged to visit Peter Dunk's house where the current vogue was to play a board game called "Dover Patrol". Also as the following day (Friday) was half-term holiday it wasn't considered too bad for me to have a later night. The plan therefore was for me to go on to the Boathouse at 9.30 pm.

'By the time I left Peter's place in Bushwood Road around 100 German bombers were already over England. As I walked past Kew Pond and on to the Green, sirens began in the far distance and shortly after the local sirens were in full swing.

The Boathouse, photographed from Kew Bridge by the Americans

'By the time I was at the bridge the siren was growling as it slowly died away. Already in the distance I could hear gunfire, so naturally I started to trot. When I eventually reached the doors of the Boathouse the gunfire was still far away. Passing through the heavy blackout curtains I poked my head into the bar. I waved to the family and my uncle signalled for me to go over to the kitchen.

'Passing through one of the two swing doors I was greeted by two female members of staff, one of whom I knew from previous visits. There were also two American servicemen who appeared to be well acquainted with the two girls. My father arrived with the grapefruit drink and I settled back to enjoy it. For a while everything was fine.

'Suddenly it was as though a gun battery was in the car park. The windows rattled as the barrage increased. A stick of bombs fell. One hit the centre of the bridge, two exploded in the river and the last fell near a surface shelter to the rear of the Pier House Laundry, in Strand on the Green.

'The crash of the explosions rocked the kitchen and at that moment I saw a blue flashing to my right. I imagined that I was caught in the explosion and in sheer panic fled. The nearest exit was a door to the rear of the kitchen. Rushing through I found myself in a dark passage. There was a door at the end which I discovered was firmly locked. Even as I rattled the door there was a thud on the outside and a flickering blue light showed beneath the door.

'With no chance of an exit I returned to the kitchen. In the far corner of the kitchen an incendiary bomb was cracking away with whitish blue pieces showering over the hard glazed floor. One of the American servicemen was lying flat on the tiles. He was, as I recall, yelling at the others to do likewise in case the device contained an explosive charge.

'In the doorway was my mother shouting for me to get out. Water was coming through the ceiling just above the door but my mother appeared completely oblivious to the fact that she was getting wet. Having got back into the lounge it was now almost empty of customers. There was a commotion behind the bar where possibly another device was burning. Together with my family, we reached the car park. The noise of the guns and aircraft passing overhead was accompanied by the explosions of bombs falling some distance away. The sky was full of orange lights that floated downwards. Later it was reported that over eighty flares had been dropped.

'There appeared to be plenty of activity on the far side of the bridge and the signs were that Brentford was having a hectic time. My father and uncle practically lifted my grandmother from the ground and we all hurried across the car park. One or two unexploded incendiaries were lying around and we were careful to avoid them.

'By the car park entrance a solitary vehicle had been struck by a firebomb. The device was lodged between the bonnet and wing. The motorist was tackling this with what appeared to be a quart bottle of beer. Up on the Green a number of twinkling lights marked the spots where bombs were burning on the grass. Far away to the right and closer to Ferry Lane flames were coming from the top floor of a building. With all the flashes the sky was completely lit up.

'When we reached the bridge there was obviously something burning over on Strand on the Green. Further over there was a red glow in the sky where a fair sized fire had taken hold. We dashed below ground into the shelter. In fact this was the first time I had taken cover on Kew Green since September 1940.

'Eventually the all-clear sounded and we emerged and made our way to Priory Road. There was now nothing to be seen around the Green. All the incendiaries and the fire further over had obviously been dealt with. There was still a glow in the sky from a fire further east but apart from this complete darkness. The Boathouse was still there which rather surprised me. The only evidence that could be seen was a number of different coloured patches on the roof of the building where the bombs had pierced through. In the meantime a number of the lads had managed to obtain thermite from some of the unexploded devices. This however proved very difficult to ignite.

'I recall that the events left me feeling a little light headed. This took a day or two to calm down. I suppose these days it would be called traumatic stress.'

Oddly, this terrifying attack did not rate so much as an entry in the Kew ARP records, perhaps because the great majority of the bombs that evening fell on the north side of the river, with a succession of 50 KG HE and Phosphorous bombs. However, the Chiswick ARP records confirm Ron Draper's account, recording that the first three HE bombs hit Stile Hall Road, Kew Bridge station, and Thames Road, that two more fell in the river, and that the last one 'exploded ten feet from the eastern parapet of the central span of Kew Bridge'. Ron recalls that the blast was largely absorbed by a brick-built army post that stood in the centre of the bridge – probably used by Minewatchers, who manned the bridges to watch out for mines that might be dropped and be floating in the river. The scars of bomb splinters can still be seen on the plaques on the parapets.

On the same night Kew Gardens were also hit especially hard, with seven bombs. The *Journal of the Kew Guild* somewhat wearily reported that the Temperate House had lost much of its glass for the third time since the start of the war. The staff was used to the chore of clearing up the mess before re-opening for the visitors. 'Canvas was hastily put up along the sides of the house pending the work of re-glazing. For about a week after this raid the Gardens were closed on account of five unexploded bombs which had to be removed by the bomb-disposal squads.'

The Gardens had been hit regularly during the Blitz: Ray Desmond in *Kew*, his magisterial history of the Gardens, reports that 'a total of some 30 high explosives had fallen within the Gardens, breaking glass in the Temperate House, the Palm House, North Gallery and the Museum facing the pond, and severely damaging the Tropical Water Lily House.'

The Sandbagged Herbarium (Photo courtesy Jim Keesing)

The *Journal*'s account is typically phlegmatic: people were now used to keeping things going in what must have been very frightening and frustrating times. Although visitor numbers did fall – at Easter, for instance, from 71,000 in 1939 to 38,888 in 1941, according a report in the *Thames Valley Times* – the Gardens remained open throughout the war, give or take the odd closure to clear up bomb damage or clear out time bombs. Otherwise it was a matter of 'business as usual'.

CHAPTER 3 – *How we lived then*

War on the battlefield has been described as long stretches of boredom punctuated by brief moments of sheer terror. From 1939 to 1945 much the same could have been said of the war on the Home Front. Kew residents certainly needed battlefield courage to face the terrors of the Blitz and the later raids by the V bombs, but the majority of the war years demanded courage of a different sort – a kind of bloody-minded refusal to give in to the discomforts and disappointments of a life disrupted by emergency regulations, by persistent shortages and by the imposition of rationing.

There was a host of new regulations, dating back to 1938 and earlier. Kew residents mostly recall those that especially restricted their freedom – such as having to carry gas masks wherever you went, and the need for blackouts. For much of the war gas masks had to be carried, and there were special gasproof cradles for babies. Gas was considered a major threat. Pat Thomas remembers her father, who was an air-raid warden 'out walking in his full regalia – yellow oilskins and gas mask and rattle. His rattle was to warn people there might be a gas attack. We put wet blankets over our front doors in case of gas. Outside the Coach and Horses at one stage, there was a lorry filled with poisoned gas. We all had to queue up with our gas masks on and walk quickly taking a little sniff at it so we knew what it would be like. I was petrified and refused to go by.'

Evelyn Tyrer, a teenager at that time living in Lawn Crescent, was active first as a fire watcher and then as Air-Raid Warden. Her younger brother was a 'messenger', taking messages to and from the ARP post. 'Fire watchers were organised in teams of four, because that was the number required to use a stirrup pump: one to pump, one to direct the hose and two to fetch buckets of water to keep the pump supplied. There were forty-two houses in Lawn Crescent, and three or four teams. The choice for the fourth member for my mother's team lay between a ninety-year-old man next door or my eleven-year-old sister; it was decided that the eleven-year-old would be the better pumper. In the windows of the house were displayed notices which said "stirrup pump kept here".'

Later Evelyn and a friend volunteered as Air-Raid Wardens. 'I was assigned to D post in the grounds of St Luke's church in the Avenue. The head of D unit was full time and paid; the rest of the staff were part-time volunteers. I never had to deal with an incident but there was still plenty to do: gas-mask practice, checking the blackout, checking on available shelters and checking on sleep-in tickets. These were slips of paper placed in a green box attached to our front door to say who was sleeping in each house that night; often the occupiers would add a note saying "..... away today".'

Windows had to be blacked out, and you could be taken to court for persistent offences. The *Thames Valley Times* reported several cases in which Kew householders were fined up to £2 for 'causing a light to be displayed'. There were also cases where the blackout caused its own hazards, as when a Mr White of Priory Road 'fell into a trench, constructed for ARP purposes and broke 3 ribs....On behalf of the defendants it was stated that there was a trench in the path which had been covered over with planks.... If he had kept to the path, he would not have fallen in. The Bench decided no case to answer – dismissed.'

Ron Draper recalls that money could be made out of the blackout: 'During blackouts it was complete darkness. There were no streetlights and vehicles had headlights with slatted discs fitted over. On a foggy day in a blackout it was chaotic. There weren't many private cars, but plenty of buses, commercial vehicles and army convoys coming through. Armed with a torch, you and a couple of lads could earn a penny or two pocket money, guiding vehicles round the Green up the road to Richmond. Those fogs were thick and yellow, so you couldn't see your hand in front of your face.'

There was a mass of other regulations that people learned to live with, most of them now long forgotten. Fortunately, however, one resident, Mrs Drew of Ennerdale Road, made a careful collection of all the leaflets that were delivered to every household both before and during the war. She also kept an immaculate account of every bill she paid. This invaluable record of life in Kew at that time has been preserved by her granddaughter, Marian Mollett, who is known for her own contribution to the community as the former Chair of the Richmond Parish Lands.

Marian's grandmother had had an interesting, peripatetic, life. By birth she was part British, part German. In the First World War, she lived in Mexico with her husband, Arthur Drew, a British businessman. On his death in 1920, she moved back to Germany with two young children. As she and her brother were totally opposed to the Nazi regime, they left to settle in Britain just before Munich. Her elder son was in the Civil

19

Service, and would eventually be knighted for his services, as Sir Arthur Drew. Her younger son, Harry, joined the British army, was captured in North Africa, and later escaped.

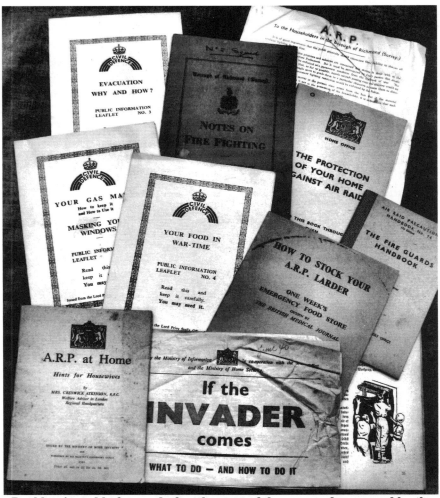

Booklets issued before and after the start of the war, and preserved by the Drew family. The picture (bottom right), giving advice on installing blackout, is from a German booklet of 1938.

Meanwhile she and her brother had settled in Ennerdale Road. They were both admirably conscientious over studying the regulations and attending any meetings called by the ARP. Ironically, in their determination to keep every relevant document, they managed to preserve in their archive not only the British leaflets but also a German leaflet they received in 1938, just before they left for England. This contained almost the same information and advice on matters such as blackout as that being issued in Britain, both countries being equally – and correctly – convinced that war was on its way.

Some of the material in this chapter is culled from Mrs Drew's accounts, as she and her brother recorded their living costs in immense detail. They were clearly among the better-off residents at that time, but for essentials they were just as constricted by rationing as the poorest in Kew. They were, for instance, for ever battling to reduce their fuel consumption to enable them to heat their detached house and still remain within the official guidelines on coke, electricity and gas. As their annual expenditure on fuel was £168 in 1939, and only £99 in 1945, they seem gradually to have mastered the problem, as others had to do in their smaller houses.

Rationing

Shortages of food and rationing were an even greater burden, and these would last long beyond the end of the war. Each person in every household was issued with a ration book. 'Rations' covered those essential foods of which a certain set amount was available weekly for each person in the household. Both items and quantities varied throughout the war. Tea, sugar, fats and meat were rationed from 1940; eggs, cheese and jam from 1941; sweets from 1942. Bread was not rationed until after the war. When restrictions were at their most severe (early in 1941) each adult was allowed each week 4oz bacon or ham, 2oz butter, 4oz margarine, 2oz cooking fats, 2oz cheese and only 1/10d worth of meat. Later in the war, 'Points' were introduced for a variety of more exotic foods such as processed meat and tinned salmon. 'A lady sat in a booth in the corner of every shop and she cut out your coupon,' Roy Featherstone remembers.

Clothes could only be bought if you had 'Clothing Coupons'. Early in the war, you were allowed 66 points. In 1942 this was cut to 48 and then to 36 in 1943, and in 1945 to 24. In 1945, an overcoat (wool and fully lined) took 18 coupons; a man's suit 26-29 (according to lining); men's shoes 9, women's shoes 7; a woollen dress 11. Children aged 14-16 got 20 extra coupons. People had extra coupons for work clothes, such as overalls for factory work.

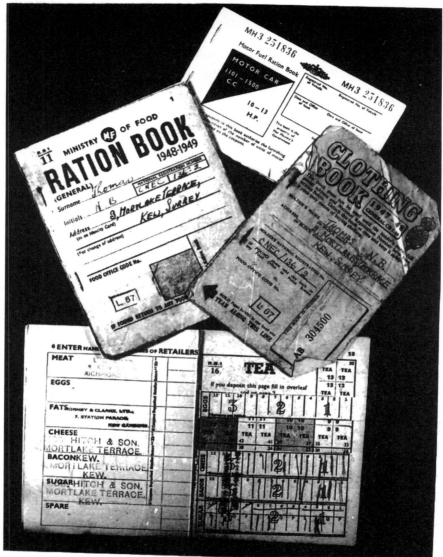

Ration Books, Clothing and Petrol Coupons (Photo Pat Thomas)

There was still the chance that something out of the ordinary might appear in some shop, so long as you were prepared to queue for it. 'There was immense excitement when the Richmond greengrocers got some bananas, but we were only allowed two of them each,' Pat Thomas recalls. Bananas were certainly out of the ordinary throughout the war.

So were oranges and lemons, and fancy cakes. Fish too was in such short supply that you had to queue.

There were, however, opportunities to supplement the rations. It was possible to buy a meal in a British Restaurant. 'The British Restaurants were sort of government sponsored soup kitchens,' David Colley recalled. 'They were manned by the WVS. St Luke's Hall [at the junction of Dudley and Sandycombe Roads] had one. For sixpence you could get an enormous midday meal.' Otherwise families had to improvise and so did some of the shops: Mike Wilsden recalls that his grandfather, who ran the bakery in North Road (later to be run by Mr Fix), used to produce the most delicious apple turnovers. They were made out of parsnips, with just a flavouring of apple juice.

It has been argued that the strict rationing of food probably produced a fitter generation of children that those brought up in today's more generous circumstances. Certainly, there was an immense increase in the amount of land used for vegetables. 'Everybody grew vegetables in their garden,' according to Judy Strange, 'lettuce, spinach, beans, tomatoes, anything we could.' At the same time space was made available for new allotments on Kew Green (but not on the cricket square), in North Sheen Rec, and between the towpath and Kew Barracks, to supplement the existing plots on Short Lots. The Royal Botanic Gardens followed suit by turning over the lawns in front of Kew Palace to potatoes, and offering practical advice to the public by way of demonstration allotment plots.

In the First World War, as described in Chapter 1, Kew played a surprisingly prominent role in raising money to send cigarettes to the front. In the Second World War Kew was similarly involved in supporting the troops, though more modestly as part of what was then a countywide campaign. There were those who went door to door selling stamps for Savings Certificates, and raising funds for the building of planes and ships. Richmond Borough celebrated the 50th jubilee of its incorporation by raising £5000 for a Spitfire, and during 'Warship Week' in 1941 residents gave over £250,000 to adopt HMS *Richmond*. In 1943 they went even further by contributing £460,000 to the Wings for Victory campaign (enough to buy 23 Mosquitoes.)

These campaigns were complemented by a new enthusiasm for recycling that covered everything from paper and rags to aluminium pots and pans. It was encouraged by the exhortation to 'Play your part in the war effort', a phrase that excused almost any break with tradition. It covered, for instance, the removal of the railings from North Sheen Rec and from most of Kew Green, though not from the small triangle by the main gate of the Gardens. This was apparently because this was royal land, an odd exemption in view of Queen Mary's childhood affection for Kew and her later well-known enthusiasm for collecting scrap. (At Badminton in Gloucestershire she was renowned for seizing ploughs left unguarded in the fields, and they had to be returned surreptitiously to the indignant farmers who did not share Her Majesty's determination to reverse the biblical injunction to turn swords into ploughshares.)

Some of the great stock pile of scrap iron collected throughout Britain was intended for those factories buildings planes, and of course Kew had an interest in this business. As in the First World War, the industrial site between the river and West Park Avenue was producing aircraft, or at least the fuselages for them. In the Second World War, there were about 200 workers there, many of them women. Valerie Horwill worked in the office there as a teenager, and recalls that the factory stretched the full length of the current retail park, with its air-raid shelters built alongside Kew Meadows Path. It was still run by Chrysler's American/British management team, but it no longer built lorries; it built the rear end of Halifax bomber fuselages

A service at Chryslers, with the Halifax fuselages in the background

This was the biggest industrial operation in Kew, but there were other smaller businesses, known as 'shadow factories', which made less well publicised contributions to the war effort, with the minimum of publicity, to ensure that they would not be identified and bombed by the enemy. Typical of these was Grampian Reproducers in Station Avenue, which shifted from making parts for radios to submarine detectors. This was sensitive work and Rosemary Caple, whose family who ran the Cherry Tree café in Station Parade, remembers that there was a uniformed guard stationed in Station Avenue, known as Victor. He was a cheerful character, but was clearly there to prevent unauthorised access to the factory.

Outsiders

Oddly those who were children in Kew talk very little about evacuees. Yet Kew played host to a considerable number of them, both from the East End during the Blitz and from overseas. Joyce Perkins, who was working in the post office on Kew Green in 1940, recalls the arrival of the first wave. They came dramatically upriver, on coal barges. She remembers how they sat on the pavement of Maze Road, waiting for someone to take them in. Those with spare rooms had to accept them.

It must have been an embarrassing occasion both for the householders and the evacuees, but Joyce was struck by the eagerness with which the host families rushed to the post office to claim their payment. She recalls that the weekly payment then was 5s for adults and 2/6 for children. [The official rate varied throughout the war, but it was eventually settled at 10s 6d per week for the 5-10 year olds, going up to 16s 6d for those over 17.] She recalls that many of the evacuees stayed on in Kew after the Blitz, and indeed after the war. They seem to have quickly become part of the community. If that is so, that may explain why their arrival made so little lasting impression on their contemporaries. Ron Draper, for instance, who arrived a little later from the East End, to live in Haverfield Gardens with his uncle and aunt, certainly became a close friend of his fellow Kew teenagers, and has remained so ever since.

The *Thames Valley Times* of 30th May 1941 published details from the annual report of the King's School, Kew, which referred to the problems caused by air raids and the loss of the Green to play on. Then it pointed out that out of a roll of 206, no fewer than 47 of the pupils were recent arrivals in Kew. Of these, 25 were 'evacuees from Stepney', presumably those who came up river in the coal barges. The others were 'Belgian and Czech refugees'. These are said to have been settled mostly in Priory Road, which had been largely deserted early in the war by the owners, who had themselves chosen 'voluntary evacuation' by moving way out into the countryside. (The King's School calculated that they had lost 35 from their roll by this voluntary evacuation.)

Despite all of this coming and going, the new regulations, the rationing, it is remarkable how much of life went on as before. There were still fairs on the Green at Easter. In 1941 the press reported that Mr Beech's fairground, 'which was bombed a few months ago, had the big roundabout, the swing boats, and some of the sideshows in full activity again, although it is not nearly as extensive as it was. The coconut shy had the coconuts replaced with wooden balls, while instead of a coconut, the cry was "Every time you win you get a 6d savings stamp."' In 1942 the press noted that numbers at the Kew Fair were down on the days before the war, but the number of communicants was up at St Anne's.

There were also plenty of cases to fill their court reports, several of them from Kew. There were the usual petty thefts, but there were also some less familiar, more disconcerting, cases to report on. These involved local people who were determined not to obey the new wartime regulations, on grounds of conscience. Three of these conscientious objectors came from Kew, and each offered a distinctive defence to a charge of refusing to register for fire watching duties. One from Sandycombe Road said that his refusal was based on his experiences as a soldier in the last war. One from Defoe Avenue said that imprisonment as a conscientious objector in the previous war had not changed his mind. One from Gainsborough Road pleaded pacifism on religious grounds. Their sentences varied between two and six months imprisonment with hard labour. These three would have been exceptions to the rule. Most 'Conchies' applied for registration, and agreed to undertake war work. We know of at least one in Kew who took this step. There may well have been others. It is easy to forget how tolerant of dissent Britain was in wartime: over 60,000 applied for registration.

It is, however, equally easy to forget that not everyone was comfortable with the way that life had changed with the advent of war. Britain had for centuries been run on the assumption that class differences had to be preserved. Yet in wartime – more especially with the arrival of the less class-conscious American troops – the old distinctions seemed out of date. One resident recalls that 'many of the houses were divided into flats or single rooms and housed somewhat uneasily a wide range of society from families of relatively senior officers, well-heeled widows and single women to quite poor families, many of other ranks with larger numbers of children. This put stresses on neighbourly relations as many struggled to maintain a distance and pre-war "standards". This meant that many people did not go into the Anderson shelters in spite of being very frightened by the bombing. They were also rather smelly and uncomfortable. The lack of social interaction was also revealed when men came home on leave and took their wives to relax at the local Kew Gardens Hotel. Whatever the developing social camaraderie that existed amongst serving service personnel, the division between public and saloon bars ensured that neighbours in the same house did not mix there either.'

CHAPTER 4 – YANKS IN LIMEYLAND

A major change came to Kew during the war when the largest local employer closed its doors at the end of Ruskin Avenue, and its place was taken by a large number of soldiers from our most important war-time ally and then by an even larger number of enemy prisoners of war. The exodus was perhaps generally felt like the ebbing of the tide; the influx, to some, was going to be a tidal wave.

Almost all of the Ruskin Avenue site, where the National Archives now stand, was historically part of Mortlake Parish and in 1800 was given over to pasture, probably fattening livestock for the London market. Later it was used for market gardening. In 1892 it became part of Richmond Borough. The houses in Ruskin Avenue itself and Defoe Avenue were built from 1905 onwards. In 1916, during the First World War, it was decided to centralise the administration of the new Unemployment Insurance, and the Ruskin Avenue site (together with the cauliflowers growing on it) was bought, and a huge one-storey complex, covering two and a half acres, was built. One of the rooms, the Ledger room, which was 380 feet long and 100 feet wide, was thought to be the largest room in London; a second of almost equal size was used for the valuation of the Unemployment Fund. The offices were 'strongly, though not elaborately built', but with modern electricity, a central heating system and kitchens for a canteen.

Although this new 'Claims and Record Office' was originally intended to employ between 800 and 900 people, the work expanded and the building was extended, so that by November 1919 there were 350 men and 1,237 women working there. Over the next twenty years the total number nearly doubled to a figure of just under 3,000 employees, 1,596 men and 1,371 women. At the start of the Second World War, having rejected a suggestion that the whole office might be relocated to 'somewhere between say Bletchley and Crewe', the Government decided to close the whole office. A few months later in early 1940 they decided to reopen the office in Acton on a reduced scale, but the Ruskin Avenue site remained vacant.

It does not appear to have had a particular use at first. It may have been used as a transit camp for various units of the British Army, but none stayed long. Harry Abbett, who worked as a paper boy for the Marigold shop, which was on the corner of Forest Road, remembers delivering papers at the site to some soldiers, probably from the Guards, whose job was to guard the Kew railway bridge. It has been suggested that they were from the Scots Guards and that probably it was only a platoon. The Coldstream Guards were possibly there later. Then, when the Americans entered the war after Pearl Harbor, Ruskin Avenue was earmarked for one of the bases they were going to need in England.

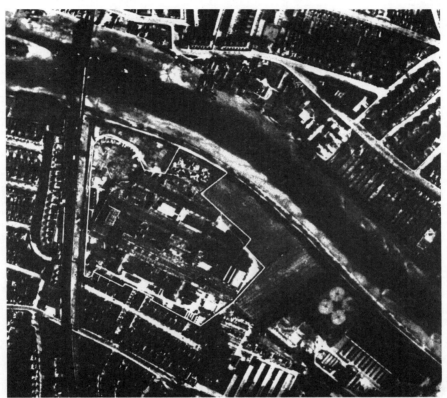

**An aerial photograph of Kew Barracks, taken by the Americans, and
showing the extent of the three long buildings**

The first Americans arrived on Monday 7th September 1942; they were 'B' Company of the 660th Engineers Topographical Battalion of the US Army. They were welcomed, first by a band of the Irish Guards in kilts at Richmond station, then by the Coldstream Guards with a meal in Ruskin Avenue and finally by a Luftwaffe air raid just after they had gone to bed. 'C' Company and part of the Headquarters Company crossed the Atlantic in the *Queen Mary* and reached England on 13th December. In

April 1943 nearly a 100 'newbies' came from Engineering school in the USA, and finally 'A' Company and the rest of the Headquarters Company joined them on 12th August 1943 to complete the Battalion. Although there was a core that formed a 'settled' population, many men came and went over the two-year period that the Americans were on the site. Various individuals and small groups joined or left the battalion. In addition, numerous other units of the US Army passed through in transit, while others were there for longer periods including parts of 952nd Engineers, 12th Air Force, and 62nd Engineers. Moreover, there were still British institutions using part of the Ruskin Avenue site: the Post Office occupied a considerable space with their Stores Depot and the Ministry of Works had a workshop there.

The camp was large: it contained not merely extensive working areas as well as sleeping quarters and all the administrative offices, but also a mess-hall – they inherited a modern kitchen and canteen from the Claims and Record Office – NAAFI, reading and game rooms, showers, barber shop, gymnasium, chapel, doctor's and dentist's surgeries. The size and layout of the camp made it extremely confusing. 'The maze at Hampton Court ran a poor second to the seemingly endless criss-cross of hallways. Each newcomer required at least two days to find his sleeping area or the NAAFI.' (This quote, and many others in this chapter, are taken directly from the GIs' 'Souvenir Books'.)

The task of the 660th Engineers was to make maps for the invasion of France. The battalion consisted of over 900 men: 878 other ranks and some 40 officers were on the pay roll in England in December 1943. The battalion was divided into 4 companies. Headquarters Company, which was the smallest unit with 20 officers and 108 other ranks, was concerned with Administration, Operations, Transportation and Supply. 'A' Company's job was surveying. Its 180 men 'lived at Kew, but trained in the English countryside and along the coast. Groups were sent to train at various sites which had similar terrain to areas across the Channel.' The biggest company was 'B' Company with 337 men and 8 officers; as its work was photomapping, the technical heart of the battalion, most of the men in the company were specialist trained technicians: only a quarter of them were privates or privates first class, whereas they formed half the other companies. Finally, 'C' Company, which was concerned with reproduction (printing the maps) consisted of 243 men, who were stationed for at least part of the time in Cheltenham.

The process of making maps was difficult, complicated and technical. Traditional mapmakers usually began with a careful field survey but, as France was occupied by the enemy, the Americans started with photographs brought back by reconnaissance flights, generally by Lockheed P-38s fitted with five cameras with lenses of different focal lengths able to take photos at 25,000ft every few seconds. The flights criss-crossed the area to be mapped taking multiple photographs. The job of photomapping was to transform these photographs into maps. Although they used the most advanced technology, such as the Multiplex stereoscopic plotter, this work depended on the patient skill and the meticulous precision of the men. They produced over two thousand maps, covering most of northern France, and town plan mosaics of 28 towns to identify bombing targets.

The Photomappers at work

31

One of their most important jobs was to locate and produce detailed maps of possible landing strips, essential for bringing in troops and supplies after D-Day. Working from photographs from low-altitude reconnaissance flights, they made maps with 5-foot contours of 118 possible airfields. The engineers who later built the landing strips were amazed that such accurate maps had been made without a surveying party working on the ground. They also made four relief models of coastal sites, crucial for planning and preparation, each taking about 6 weeks to construct. The first was of the Devon coast near Barnstable for an invasion exercise; two were of hypothetical coastlines; the last and most important was of Omaha Beach. The maps themselves were reproduced in vast numbers of impressions by 'C' Company with its processing, camera and press sections. Using the most up-to-date technology, including Webendorfer 'Big Chief' offset presses, they produced 8,269,250 impressions in the single month of June 1944.

This huge amount of work required three eight-hour shifts a day, except for Sunday. All of this was very typical of a modern army and of the USA: the most modern technology combined with human industry, ingenuity and skill forming one small element in a vast behemoth. All of this was to produce maps – and maps were vital. The men appreciated the importance of their work; and they did it seriously; but what they could not appreciate were the irksome aspects of Army life. Despite the fact that by the time they left Kew some men had been in the Army for three years, they did not feel themselves to be full-time military soldiers: they were still civilians who happened to be in the Army. There were exercises and long hikes, rifle training and drill in the Old Deer Park, sometimes up to four hours after a full shift's work. 'Why?' they asked. 'A CBS (Central Base Section) order', was the inevitable reply. Indeed, the orders did come down from the very top, from Eisenhower and Marshall, who were determined to turn civilians into a proper military machine. Nevertheless, at Kew the GIs were sceptical when Lieutenant Combs constantly repeated, 'You men must get HARD.' Then there were inspections: Full Field Inspections on Kew Green with everything precisely laid out, causing the British civilian onlookers to comment, 'Jolly good – but why?' Back at camp there were more inspections, guard duty and guard mount, then the various forms of cleaning and tidying; the Broom and Mop routine, KP (Kitchen Police, cleaning up the kitchen), the Trash Detail, etc. It all made for 'chicken' – or 'chickenshit', which is what they thought of it.

The 'B' company souvenir book, *Our Mapping Years*, gives very brief biographies of 358 men, which enables us to get some information about who these Americans were. The first salient fact was that they were nearly all enlisted men, civilians, not Army men. The USA before the war had a very small army; from 1941 General Marshall had to create a huge new army from civilians. Less than ten percent of 'B' company were Regular Army soldiers and most of these had joined after 1940. Only the Commanding Officer, Colonel Abell, who was a West Pointer, and a handful of others had much pre-war service. One Master Sergeant had joined up in 1930 and one private in 1926.

The answer to General Eisenhower's standard question, 'Where do you come from, soldier?' was in this case, 'All over'. They came from 40 out of the 49 states (counting Washington DC as a state), but the spread was not even. Of these 40 states half only sent one, two or three individuals. A few states sent large numbers: about one-fifth of the number came from Pennsylvania (75 men) and New York (73 men); next came Ohio with 31 men. If we group states by region, half of the men came from the Mid-Atlantic states (although these states contained only a quarter of the US population in 1940); another quarter came from the Mid-West, so that only a few came from the rest of the country, the South or the West or New England. Essentially they came from the most industrialised parts of the country, which is to be expected, given the nature of their work. They did not come necessarily from big cities; only a quarter came from the biggest cities (i.e. cities with a population of more than a quarter of a million in 1940): 25 came from New York – by far the largest city in the USA at the time, 10 came from Cleveland and 8 from Philadelphia. Most came from smaller towns.

Few, however, came from the countryside, although a quarter of the population then lived on farms. We know the former civilian jobs of 185 men; only 4 were farmers (3 from the South). Only three had direct map-making experience – one for the Department of Commerce, one for the American Meteorological Society and one as a "topo engineer" – but many had clearly relevant experience: 20 had been draftsmen; 17 were artists, architects or designers; 13 were engineers and 8 worked in photography. These had been sent to specialist schools, for example at the University of Kentucky, to gain topographical expertise. The 24 who had been students were also suitable for such training. The rest (the remaining 60%) were drawn from all kinds of background: some worked in steel, one in show business; there was a footwear craftsman and an assistant golf pro, a mortician and a hosiery salesman. Overall, they were not typical enlisted men; in Norman Longmate's book, *The G.I's. The Americans in Britain,* a British acquaintance describes them as a highly sophisticated unit consisting largely of 'artists, musicians and scene-painters in Hollywood'.

If we look at their names, while two thirds seem to be British or Irish, one third are that typical mixture that reflects the immigration patterns of the late 19th and early 20th century, being German and eastern European, French and Italian, Swedish, Jewish and Armenian. Many were given nicknames, showing their camaraderie. Most of these were abbreviations of their first names or their surnames. Others reflected their origins (Irish, Greek, Scotty, the Rebel, Greaseball (*sic*!)), and some their physical characteristics (Curly, Red, Porco and Porky, Stumpy, Tiny, Rabbit); some their age (the Kid, Pop, Pappy, the Old Man), while others referred to their proficiency either in sports (Fearless, Elbow, the White Hope) or in other respects (Boogie Woogie, Hoofer, the Sponge, Bing, Leather-lung). Whereas we can understand some references (Groucho, Hollywood, Scruffy, the Professor, Stinky), others are more obscure (Steamboat, Kimono, Foxhole, Vesicant). What they do show is their individuality; even though there were very few Hispanics and no blacks, and even though they were all men, what is noticeable to us, and what must have been striking to them, is their diversity. For the US Army, however, they were all Americans, just as for the British they were all simply 'the Americans', at least until some got to know them better.

General Marshall was determined that the soldiers' welfare would always be a high priority. Thus they were well paid, well fed, well entertained. Sports were encouraged with tournaments between units: they played basketball in the camp and baseball on Kew Green or the Old Deer Park. Tours of various stars were arranged: in January 1944 there was an ice-skating programme at the Sports-Drome across Richmond Bridge, and six months later there was an exhibition of bouts of boxing, the chief star being Staff-Sergeant Joe Louis, the great World Heavyweight Champion, who later visited Ruskin Avenue. The American Red Cross established clubs for American service men, particularly in the centre of London but also in other localities: they took over Trumpeters' House in Richmond, where they could relax or eat or play badminton or even dance to Pat Barella's band.

The entrance to Kew Barracks

The British Government and the local authorities made efforts to welcome the Americans. The Richmond Council of Social Service helped set up Trumpeters' House and started an Information Bureau. In October 1942 there was a baseball game between US and Canadian troops at Richmond Athletic Ground in front of a big crowd. The Mayor of Richmond was present in his robes and pitched the first ball. In May 1943 there was a special showing for the 660th Engineers of the Warner Brothers musical *Yankee Doodle Dandy* (with its 'gay music, sincere pathos & a splendid message of patriotism') at the Ritz Cinema. The Mayor welcomed them and 'hoped the public would go out of their way to make them as happy as possible during their stay'. Captain Locke replied that 'the English people were not only their allies – and very good allies – but what was more important that they were their friends, and very good friends.' The following week the 660th were guests of honour and led the 3rd anniversary parade of 63rd Surrey (Richmond) Battalion of the Home Guard on Richmond Green.

Many were assiduous tourists, taking photographs whenever they could, not merely visiting the sights of London, but travelling on furlough to Stratford-upon-Avon or Cornwall or Scotland. Mostly, however, they spent their time locally and there met British people. Some British people actually worked at the camp, particularly Miss Cox and her NAAFI girls, including Olive, Mae and Nora who pushed tea-carts round the workshops at 10am, 2.30 and 8pm for the 10-minute NAAFI breaks. Longmate records in his book that 'The manageress of the NAAFI

35

canteen serving the 660th Engineers at Kew gardens, accustomed to dealing with the rigidly disciplined men of the Coldstream Guards, remembers how the crowds round the counter clamouring for coffee and biscuits, meant that, "the girls could not serve the men at the back, so I asked them if they would line up during the busy breaks. They said they were not Limeys, so I pulled down the shutters and said I would open them again when they did what I asked. They booed and catcalled, then all of a sudden there was silence. I looked thinking the canteen was empty. Instead they were all in a line and we never had any more trouble."'

Even before the first GIs arrived at Ruskin Avenue, on 12th August 1942 the *Thames Valley Times* had been urging the people of Richmond to strengthen 'the great bond of free and democratic institutions....So, when you have the opportunity, ask an American into your home. You don't need to worry because there isn't too much food to spare, because you cannot have guests waited on in the grand manner. He doesn't want to have a fuss made of him; he just wants to feel something of the informality and comfort of the home life he enjoys so much in the States.' It warned, however, 'Don't be surprised if you find that the Americans are "different".' Many took up this request; at Christmas that year 300 American soldiers were welcomed in local homes. The Americans appreciated the efforts made by their hosts in the difficult conditions of rationing, while the hosts were grateful for tins of salmon or pineapple. Many friendships were formed, some to last many years.

The word people seem to use most often in recalling the Americans is 'generous'. They were generous, open-hearted, friendly and warm. They were especially generous to children – sweets and, of course, chewing gum. (For older people, it was cigarettes.) The high points were their Christmas parties. In 1943 they invited 300 children whose fathers had been killed or were prisoners or were abroad to a party in the camp. Everybody had an 'Uncle' and there were games like tag, leap-frog and potato races and cartoons with Mickey and Donald and Pluto, and Santa was in his grotto (actually Corporal Savino) and there was a sing-song and you followed the words with a bouncing ball on the screen and there was food and tea and cakes and ICE CREAM and at the end everyone went home with a present and a bag of candy (the men had saved their rations and contributed presents). The Mayor said the children would always remember it – and indeed they still do. One of those children, Len Timms, is one those who have persistently – and now successfully – argued that Kew should record its thanks to the American visitors.

Julia Lee, Head Mistress of the Vineyard Infants' School, was moved to verse, which was published in the *Richmond and Twickenham Times*,

> Hurrah! for the U.S.A. Forces
> We met in the building at Kew,
> Who gave us the loveliest party
> We in peace time or war ever knew.
>
> Delicious the tea set before us
> Of goodies now too rarely seen;
> We really could scarcely believe it,
> 'Twas just like a wonderful dream.
>
> Three Christmas trees all gay and stately,
> And Santa Claus cheery and bright,
> The films with our dear old friend Mickey
> Were all such a thorough delight.
>
> But oh! She was fairer than fairest,
> A lovelier never was seen,
> In dainty pink robe, silver glinting,
> The exquisite young Fairy Queen.
>
> We send you our thanks, U.S Forces,
> Our thanks that are hearty and true
> For one of the very best parties
> That ever was given at Kew.

Like many British people, the Americans often spent their leisure in pubs. Spirits were in low supplies, even to their amazement Scotch; the beer was different, but they soon got used to that, although on busy days it might run out by 9 o'clock. In one souvenir book there is a map entitled 'Our Stompin' Grounds', which shows their view of Richmond and Kew. There are 60 places marked; 11 are buildings in Kew Gardens. Of the other 49, 31 are pubs, giving a comprehensive map of the pubs of Richmond and Kew during the war. Some inevitably became their favourites, and they admitted, 'The proprietors of the multi-bar Castle, the Ship and the Roebuck had their civilian customers driven off by the American Occupation forces.' If they did not want to go as far as Richmond, they patronised the four pubs on Kew Green. The most popular, however, was the Boathouse, near Kew Bridge, despite Colonel Abell's attempt to give it an Off Limits designation; it was the closest and easiest to find in the blackout. It also had a band and dancing – dancing and girls.

The GIs recalled, 'English girls dance a little differently than we. This presented a difficulty at first – in Europe the waltz is much more important than in America, and also each country has its own special dance. In Limeyland, the quick-step was THE dance. Different from the fox-trot, but fairly easy to learn. They had their own adaptation of the "Jit" for fast numbers – but after a few dances they were attempting the Jitterbug, American fashion. Anyway by D-Day most of England was jitterbugging.'

As in every dance it takes two. The Americans wanted to dance with the British girls: British girls wanted to dance with Americans, who were to write, 'Richmond became a favorite rendezvous of those especially attracted to the large and friendly female population.' The Americans were popular; they were relaxed and friendly and fun. Moreover, as so many local young men had been recruited into the services, there was a dearth of male company; the Americans filled the gap. Quite a number of these relationships developed into marriage. In one company 'one-fifth of the permanent personnel made the fatal step' here. A number married in Kew itself, including Staff Sergeant Raymond 'Curly' Vnuk who married Eva Schneider from Bushwood Road, Milford Beere and 'Chet' Czerw, 'the Polish crooner'. Most strikingly, three sisters, the Ridge girls, married three 'Kew Americans': Winifred married George Burns, Alice married Daniel McBride, and May married William Farrell. Others married women from different parts of west London; Richmond, Barnes, Chiswick, Kingsbury and Harrow.

The US military authorities were not enthusiastic about such marriages. They worried about their boys being entrapped by gold-diggers looking for a passage to the USA. Soldiers had to get permission from their Commanding Officer and had to wait a month before the wedding. (In Kew of course they were a serious bunch.) Another concern for the military was venereal disease. Americans were a ripe target for prostitutes; Central London had its rather terrifying predatory 'Piccadilly Commandos', but even Kew had its house with the camellia tree in front in Burlington Avenue, 'run by a group of women with children'. Furthermore, in wartime, sex could be casual. When the Americans were there, and later in the war, children would find along the towpath 'balloons', which they could float in the bath at home.

Cartoon from an American Souvenir Book

Bad publicity could damage relations between the US and the British Government and made both sides sensitive to problems. Cases of underage girls being with Americans or unhappily married women staying out most of the night with American soldiers, neglecting or even abandoning their children came before local courts. The case for the 660th Engineers Battalion, however, that got most publicity – both nationally and indeed internationally – concerned a Staff Sergeant who was based at Cheltenham at the time. William Thompson went to a dance in the Town Hall and met a WAAF named Nora Carpenter. She became pregnant and had not one baby, but four (one subsequently died). Unfortunately he was already married. The story of the 'Lend-Lease Daddy' was taken up by papers on both sides of the Atlantic. It did not escape the journalists' notice that Thompson's company's job was Reproduction. A furious colonel from Eisenhower's staff arrived at

Battalion Headquarters in Kew and, pounding on the desk, demanded, "Why did it have to be quadruplets?' After some time Thompson's wife agreed to a divorce and he was able to marry Nora, who had come to the USA with the three infants.

There were other cases of military indiscipline. The profit motive was probably the spur to the kitchen staff who enthusiastically sold food to any British civilians they came across. A plumber from Bushwood Avenue, who worked in the Ministry of Works workshop, which was adjacent to the kitchens in Ruskin Avenue, began by buying a chicken for his sick wife, but soon the Americans were just throwing things through his workshop window. When he was arrested he had 19 tins of sausage meat, 3 tins of spam, 10lbs of bacon, 2 hams, 6 tins of salmon, an 8lb tin of cherry jam and 15 tins of corned beef for a total value of £17-18s-6d.

Not everybody in Kew whole-heartedly approved of the Americans. Inevitably there were some irritations and some causes for tut-tutting. Landlords may have liked 'the American Occupation' of their pubs, but the locals may have had different feelings. Some disapproved of the way they roared round in their trucks. When jeeps arrived with armed men to pick up money from Barclay's Bank on the Green, one resident thought Kew had become Chicago. There was some tension among young men, because the Americans seemed to steal all the girls. Servicemen especially felt angry: the Americans were paid three times as much, had smarter uniforms, had the glamour of Hollywood and even had access to nylon stockings. The *Thames Valley Times* noted that, a month before D-Day, 'there are few outward signs of that spirit of camaraderie between "Tommies" and their American counterparts. It is rare to see a "Tommy" sharing the company of an American soldier.'

Leaving

D-day was the 6th June 1944, and with the invasion of France all the battalion's work was finally going to be used. Although their beautiful models could not prevent hell on Omaha beach and paratroopers still had to drop into the unknown, the maps played their crucial part, their importance and their accuracy constantly praised.

It was now time for the battalion to move its operations to France. A Company left Kew on 11th July as well as a small group whose job was to try to find a building for the battalion to use for their map-making work. They failed to find anything in the Cherbourg Peninsula but, as Paris was liberated on 25th August 1944, it was decided to send the battalion directly there, where they took over the modern printing works of the magazine *L'Illustration* at Bobignys. The soldiers in England were divided into 3 detachments, which were sent from Kew in fortnightly intervals – on 16th September, 1st October and 15th October; only three officers remained to hand over the building to the British authorities.

And so they left. As Betty Coldman recalled 65 years later, 'Richmond was like a ..... Richmond was empty. We all said, "Isn't it awful!"' But some Americans did return from France: a few to marry local girls, others just to see friends; many more wrote letters. Later the war brides sailed across the Atlantic to start a new life in a strange, but much more prosperous country, scattered in different states like the three Ridge sisters, Winifred in Alabama, May in Philadelphia and Alice in Long Island, New York. All that the GIs left behind after two years were the memories and, we suspect, a few reminders.

The Wedding of May Ridge and William Farrell, at St Winefride's. May's youngest sister, Doris, was bridesmaid. The other sisters (two of them already married to GIs) wore bl ack in mourning for their father, Ernest, recently killed by the V2. (Photo courtesy Joan Rundle, who can be seen, aged 2, with her mother in the doorway above her grandmother, Mrs Ridge.)

CHAPTER 5 – RUN RAGGED BY ROCKETS

In the summer of 1944, in the very month that the country was celebrating the success of D Day, the Home Front found itself suddenly subjected to a revolutionary form of air attack – the V1 flying bomb. Known also as flybombs, buzzbombs or doodlebugs, the V1s were effectively pilotless jet-propelled planes that carried high explosive. The Germans launched them from sites in France and Holland in the rough direction of their target – generally London – and their accuracy was largely dependent on the vagaries of the weather. When they ran out of fuel, there would be a sudden, shocking silence, as they glided down to earth. Then there would be a huge explosion. It was terrifying if you were in the flight-path when the engine cut out. As the V1 exploded on the surface of the ground, destruction was more widely spread than it was with those bombs that pierced the ground before exploding.

The RAF tried to shoot the doodlebugs down over the sea or the open countryside, and would on occasions deflect them by flying alongside and tipping up their wings. However, sufficient numbers got through to create terror all around London, and that of course was their aim. Hitler had developed them (and their successors, the V2s) as 'reprisal weapons' – Vergelstungswaffe – to avenge the raids on German cities and the success of D-Day landings. They would harry the south east of England without relief until the Allied troops reached their launching sites and put them out of action.

Statistically Kew was comparatively unscathed by the V1s. Only two fell on Kew – one quite early in the campaign, in June, and the other in August – but hundreds more flew over Kew causing residents to retreat day after day to the shelters they had thought would never be used again. (A total of 2419 V1s fell in the London area, but only eight fell in Richmond and Kew, in contrast to 27 in Twickenham, 13 in Brentford and 15 in Heston.) As with all others in the south east, Kew residents became expert in judging whether or not the doodlebug would land on them. They waited for the silence.

Many survivors have stories to tell of those two attacks, but few had a closer brush with death than Michael Cleave, on 26 June.

'Our family lived at the top end of Thompson Avenue, at no. 92. There were four of us – Mother and Father, my sister Ursula and myself. Ursula was six years old and I was ten.

'My father worked in an Aircraft factory along the Great West Road and my mother had part-time work helping to prepare and pack K-rations [food packages providing the daily requirement of calories and vitamins for our servicemen]. She was always home for when we returned from [Darell Road] school, which was within a quarter of a mile walking distance.

'One day, my mother took my sister and me on a shopping expedition to the Co-op Store in nearby Hammersmith. As soon as we arrived, the siren sounded and we were all ushered to the basement of the store until the attack was over. This set the pattern for the rest of the day during which we had to shelter on two further occasions – once in J.Lyons & Co. in Hammersmith and again in their Richmond branch.

'This day had an added significance for me in that it was the first time I had ever owned a plastic toy. Our mother had bought us both a gift and mine was a plastic base with a movable set of horses and jockeys which were raced by the toss of a dice – it was all of one yard long and the horses measured one inch in length. I could hardly wait to start the race!

'I was stretched out on the sitting room floor and my mother and sister were in the kitchen. My mother called me to see a low flying Spitfire coming in our direction. We had quite a lengthy back garden which was separated from a large cemetery by a four foot alleyway for rear access adjacent to an eight foot high stone boundary wall. The 'Spitfire' was approximately a mile away heading towards us and losing height rapidly. Immediately I was able to recognise it as a V1 (Doodlebug) and shouted this to my mother who picked up my sister and we all ran for the front door. (Afterwards we could not understand why it was gliding down to crash with its tail of flame still coming from its engine exhaust, for it was always a sign that a Doodlebug was gliding to explode when the tail flame cut out!!)

'As we ran we left all the doors open behind us….I reached the front privet hedge and crouched down looking back for my mother and Ursula….they ran through the front door just as the Doodlebug crashed.

'I never heard the explosion and although I have recalled these events many times over the years, I still have no idea as to the noise it made. What I can recall is the sudden billowing of the sitting room window curtains and glass, tiles and bricks flying through the air all around. I watched my mother and Ursula running down the short path towards me and was sure that they must be hit by flying debris. The roof tiles were raining down as they ran but they soon collapsed on the pavement beside me and miraculously, apart from light scratches and bruises, none of us was seriously hurt. My mother had lost one of her slippers. Mum had bought us both new school uniforms and spread them out on the settee, ready for Dad to see when he returned from work – these were never to be seen again although I did find Mum's slipper a few days later, over 100 yards away!!

'All around people, neighbours and friends, were gathering to account for each other and one lady, who lived in the house opposite and had suffered less serious damage, invited everybody to her house for a cup of tea from water boiled on an open fire.

'I had seen nothing of my friend Gordy whose parents were both out at work and his older brother still at school, so I ran to his house where the front door was missing and the gap was filled with debris from the stairs which had collapsed. I was able to squeeze through directly to their living room which was totally wrecked but the table in the middle was still standing although covered with debris. At the far side, on top of the table, was Gordy's cat. As it came towards me I could see that its eyes were crossed and that it could hardly walk. When it got near to me and as I reached for it, it fell off the table and lay dead – presumably from the blast – I shouted for Gordy as I was really frightened by now and after hearing some scratching and scuffling, I saw him emerge from under the table – we looked at each other and burst out laughing, more with relief than pleasure. His face and upper body were black. It seems that when he heard the explosion, he had ducked under the table but facing the fireplace where the ashes from the night before had sat until his parents returned from work. The blast had cleared the chimney of soot and deposited it on Gordy!! We took the cat and laid it in the front garden before going to join all the others – just as the Wardens and Fire Brigade arrived.

'It was a mystery as to where the flying bomb had actually struck and all the grown-ups were mainly concerned with checking that everybody was accounted for. At the rear of our row of houses was an 8-foot stone wall which ran the whole length of the Avenue and separated us from a large West London cemetery between Mortlake and Chiswick. In the chaos all around, Gordy and I went through a rear access alleyway to investigate. There was no evidence of the bomb actually striking any of the houses at the back but we did notice a severe crack in the cemetery wall behind the house where I lived. There was nobody in the immediate area at this stage so we decided to climb to the top of the wall to see if the V1 had come down there.

'The sight we saw was staggering. The bomb had crashed into the cemetery grounds – I will not dwell on this – but quite remarkably at the foot of the wall, on the cemetery side, was one complete wing of the Doodlebug which was riddled with bullet holes and still smouldering. We ran from the scene and told the Wardens of our discovery.

'From the adults we later learned that the theory was that the bomb was being pursued by an RAF fighter which had tried to bring it down and when the pilot saw the bomb heading for a row of houses, he shot the wing off, causing the bomb to bank round and crash and explode in the cemetery. The strong cemetery wall had also contributed to our survival by pushing the wind from the blast into the air so that it struck, mainly the upper storeys of the houses. This was the theory but we never found out for sure, or who the pilot was who saved our lives and in view of the visual evidence after the explosion, this appears to be the most logical train of events.

'We were able to move back into the house, despite the damage, as the Richmond Borough Council were quick to come round and throw tarpaulins over the damaged roof – it was just a question of salvaging what we could of the contents and waiting for the gas and electricity supply to be checked and switched on again.

'Undoubtedly our little cul-de-sac was very lucky with no deaths and few minor injuries. As children (most of us were under 11 yrs) it was a very exciting time but the effect of the blast did some amazing things, like a neighbour standing at the sink, washing up and being virtually stripped of her clothes but suffering no physical injury!

'Similarly, a full bowl of eggs standing on the windowsill of Gordy's larder, which was in the unopposed path of the blast, was untouched and the eggs were not even cracked despite the debris all around!'

The cemetery and ARP records confirm Michael Cleeve's recollection, but indicate that the V1 landed in that part of the grounds that was still in use for market gardening. It was called by the ARP either Watkins or Watkinson's Field. (The Borough of Fulham had bought the whole of the current North Sheen Cemetery in 1909, but until 1959 they let out a substantial part of it for use as market gardens.) The cemetery chapel and offices were badly damaged, and three members of staff slightly hurt.

The V1s disrupted life even more than the bombers in the Blitz, as they were mostly launched and landed in daylight, and were heralded by the scream of the sirens. However, for some children this was not unwelcome. 'With the advent of the doodlebugs,' Ron Draper recalls, 'you had sirens every ten minutes. The headmaster said at assembly; "Right lads, when you're coming to school, if you are less than half way to school and the sirens go, you must go home. If you are more than half way to school, you must come and take shelter at school." Of course, you'd walk at snail's space, because you'd know that before you got half way a siren would go off. Then it was down to the green and we'd play football.'

The second doodlebug to hit Kew hit the GI camp itself, on 27 August, just before the majority of the GIs left for France. In their history of their time in Kew, the 660th Engineers gave a vivid description of how they reacted to the first raids by the V1s in June, and to the damage inflicted on their camp in August.

They calculated that the air raid sirens sounded their warning approximately 133 times in the first fifteen days – from 15 to 30 June. 'Our ears quickly became attuned to the roar and clatter of the jet-propelled flying bombs, winging their ominous way across London. At night they were twice as terrifying with their long tail of fire streaking out behind, blazing across the sky like a fiery comet, the hellish, inhuman noise shutting out all other sound....The ringing of our warning bells for every bomb over the London area didn't help our already badly shattered nerves. It was soon discovered, however, that the buzz bomb had only one set course, and it seldom deviated from that. A plotting room was set up in the Chrysler airplane plant, just adjacent to the Claims and Records building, and the route of approaching bombs was plotted by direct wire with key spotting posts in and around London. When it was known that the bomb was headed in our general direction, a signal was given to the British watchman on duty in our building, and he immediately rang the now famous "three bells". On this signal the men would go to the shelters, but even this was not imperative, as in the days of the "real" raids. A lot of men adopted a "what-the-hell" attitude – "If it's going to hit me, it *will*, regardless of where I am!" – and stayed in bed.

'The bombs seemed to be ranging closer and closer every day, and several nearby hits blew windows out of our squad room and brought down plaster. The 660th seemed to bear a charmed existence, however, and it was always someone else in "Southern England" who were the victims. The tension mounted day by day throughout July and into August, until suddenly, on a bright Sunday morning, that which we had feared the most, finally happened. Our billets suffered a direct hit!

'It was about 20 minutes before 7 o'clock on the morning of 27 August when the sound of the three bells reverberated throughout the silent squad rooms and echoed down the long, dark hallways. The hands of the clocks were stopped at 0644 when the flying bomb struck....

Kew Barracks blasted by a doodlebug

'There was a blinding flash, and then everything went black as dust and smoke and falling debris choked the air. The tinkle of splintered glass sounded like rain on the squad room floor....The bomb had exploded almost on top of the guardroom, and every office in that wing of the building was totally demolished. Several guards were seriously injured, among these Pfc Harold Billingsley, of Hq.Co., who was hospitalized for several weeks. The Office of the Day, Lt. John Calley of Hq.Co., was killed in the O.D.'s room. In the mess hall, more than a hundred yards from the point where the V-I hit, overhead water pipes jarred loose from their inadequate moorings and struck down several men as they were eating breakfast. The most severely hurt, Sgt. Jack Portrum, also of Hq Co., died in the hospital that evening.

'When the smoke had hardly cleared, the men were salvaging beds and equipment, and were moving our squad room and all the Bn offices into the comparatively undamaged sections of the vast, sprawling building, and in a few days the battalion was back into full production.'

The Second Wave

Kew was also a victim of the second wave of rocket attacks, that of the V2s. The V2s had a more conventional rocket shape and flight path, flying at immense speed so that there was no warning that they were on their way, apart from a bang overhead as they broke the sound barrier. Consequently they initially caused confusion as well as immense destruction. The first V2 to hit Britain fell north of the Thames in Chiswick. The sixth (and the second in west London) hit Kew.

The ARP recorded that it hit Chryslers at 6.15 am on 12 September. The Borough Book of Remembrance for the civilian dead records the name of seven dead, the only one of them from Kew being Ernest Ridge. Ernest (the father of the three Ridge girls who married GIs) was a volunteer fireman. He had gone outside his post to have a cigarette when the V2 landed. Four of the other victims came from Twickenham, one from Southall and one from Gateshead. That suggests that they were all employees at Chryslers. There is no exact record of the damage done to Chryslers and its war work, but we do know that the V2 destroyed a total of eight houses in West Park Avenue.

The explosion was so huge and so unexpected that no one knew – quite literally – what had hit them. There had been no warning and no hint in the press that the Germans had launched what was then an entirely revolutionary form of warfare. One of the houses hit belonged to the Fortune family who luckily were away that night. 'It was announced as a gas explosion,' Winifred Fortune recalled 'The authorities may have known, but we didn't.' The authorities had given the same explanation for the Chiswick explosion, and it was some time before they had to admit that Chiswick and Kew had been hit by a new kind of rocket, hitherto unknown in Britain.

There are minor discrepancies between the official records and Mrs Fortune's reminiscences (recorded in an interview in the 1990s). The former listed the V2 as hitting Chryslers, and causing seven deaths, none of them apparently from the houses. Mrs Fortune recalled that it left its crater in the soft gardens at the back of the houses in West Park Avenue, and that within the Avenue 'Mr. Lumley died; Mrs. Lumley was rescued by Dr. Quipman who lived on the corner.'

The Americans' description of the damage also suggests that some victims died within the houses. They wrote that they too had heard 'wild rumors that a gas main in Chiswick had exploded. These rumors were quickly nullified when another of these terrifying "gas mains" plummeted out of the stratosphere into an open lot behind Chrysler's plant. A rescue party made up mostly from HQ men aided the Civilian Defense workers in pulling the dead and wounded from the shattered houses, and few of us will soon forget the twisted and torn bodies, innocent victims of Nazi aggression.'

One of the GIs who helped in that rescue was badly injured. This was Tony Albert, who had been befriended by the Thomas family in Kew. Pat and Roy Thomas remember visiting Tony in an army hospital and being amazed at the numbers of aircraft flying overhead on that day. Only later did they realise that they had by chance been witnessing the launch of the Allied assault on Arnhem. Tony recovered to marry his girlfriend, Helen, a land girl working then in Kew Gardens, and took her back to live in the USA.

No more V2s fell around Richmond, but they caused immense destruction elsewhere. It would be many months before the allies were able to capture and destroy the site from which the V2s were launched.

CHAPTER 6 – THE 'CO-OPERATORS'

After the Americans left the Ruskin Avenue site was not to be empty for long. For a couple of months the twenty RAF men who made up 'Number 55 Repair Unit (Buildings)' used the site. Among them was William Albert Shanks, who arrived in late November or early December 1944 and left Kew on the 10th February 1945. Their job was to carry out emergency repairs to 'houses bombed by doodlebugs' in Hackney.

In late January 1945 the site was officially designated no. 144 Italian Labour Camp; as a consequence, a large group of Italian Prisoners of War arrived and were going to stay there for nearly eighteen months until nearly a year after the end of the war. These Italians were 'Co-operators'.

In June 1943 Mussolini and his Italian fascist Government had fallen, and in September the new Italian Government joined the Allies against the Germans. Meanwhile British and American forces had invaded Italy and were to spend the rest of the war slowly fighting their way up the peninsula against the Germans, who had set up a puppet government in the north under Mussolini. Given this rather confused situation where the Italians were officially our 'co-belligerents', the British Government decided in April 1944 to make Italian POWs – there were then about 100,000 in Britain – an offer of better conditions. If they volunteered to be 'co-operators', they would be granted certain privileges and receive better treatment, although their status would remain that of Prisoners of War. Italian officers would be responsible for the internal running of the camps with Italian Carabinieri forming a Police force; they would be better paid for their work; they could go anywhere within five miles of their camp during their free time; they could to go to shops and cinemas (but not pubs or dance halls); they were given a special 'spruce green' battledress with a shoulder flash saying ITALY and the Italian flag rather than the chocolate POW uniform with its coloured patches, and officers could wear a collar and tie; they could, if invited, go to British homes. They would, however, not be allowed to marry British women. For the Government this system had the advantage of circumventing the Geneva Convention on prisoners of war: the majority of Italians were working in agriculture, because POWs were not allowed to do work that directly contributed to the war effort; but 'co-operators' would not be so restricted. Subsequently 60% of the Italian POWs volunteered to be co-operators and a number of Italian Labour Battalions were formed at camps including that at Ruskin Avenue. (Another camp was at Osterley Park.)

There were many more Italians at Ruskin Avenue than there had been Americans; in July 1945 there were 2,300; in May the following year there were 'between twelve and fifteen hundred'. As the *Stato maggiore* (Italian General Staff) ran the internal affairs of the Camp, there were only 23 British guards, with Lieutenant-Colonel H.S. Hobby of the Pioneer Corps as the Camp Commander and Captain Huber of the Royal Ulster Rifles as Interpreter. The Camp had a range of services including a chaplain, medical staff under a doctor, cooks, bakers, tailors and workshops. As the number of Italians was so large, they were packed into five large dormitories with 2-tiered bunks.

One of the Italian dormitories (Photo courtesy the Imperial War Museum)

51

Not all the Italians, however, lived all the time on site, because there was a number of outposts in different parts of London, where up to 70 men could stay. These were described as 'miniature camps, with refectories, dormitories, canteen and kitchen as in the bigger camps'. They enabled them to be nearer their place of work. Their job was to carry out repairs on bomb-damaged premises, especially those recently hit by V1s and V2s. They were sent out early in the morning to various parts of London and returned in the late afternoon. The work was clearly important and occasionally dangerous. Much of the debris was taken to Ham. On 26th July 1945 a lorry set out from the camp to take a load of debris there with three Italians sitting on the rubble in the back. It turned left into Mortlake Road and as it neared the High Park Road junction, the driver swerved to avoid a coal cart and hit a tree and a lamp post. The Italians were thrown off and Lorenzo Parmigiani, aged 41, and Felice di Fabbio, aged 25, were killed.

How were the Italians viewed in Kew? It seems that those who knew them liked them, while those who did not were suspicious or even hostile. Chief among the first group was the Vicar of St Anne's parish church on Kew Green and some members of his congregation. The Revd. Evan Hopkins with the Men's Forum of St Anne's decided in July 1945 to set up a weekly club for the Italians in the parish hall in Gloucester Road. This proved to be a great success. A hundred or even two hundred men came; they played the odd game of darts or table tennis; they looked at picture papers; they brought their own band; they ran their own canteen and thoroughly cleaned up afterwards. When the club was finally closed in March 1946, the Italians presented an oil painting of a harvest scene by one of their number to the parish by way of thanks. The vicar had also urged his congregation to invite the Italians into their homes. Mr Thomas, the Kew Green chemist, who was the principal organiser of the Men's Forum club, also had his own small social club in his house on Sundays for about a dozen men. His daughter, Pat, remembers their friendliness, their charm, their good manners and she recalls how they repeatedly asked her to play 'Vienna, city of my dreams' on her accordion. Mario Finazzi, an artist who gave the family several pictures, and some others remained friends for many years.

Winifred Percival, a Quaker from York, toured the country in her free time, visiting Italian prisoner of war camps, giving piano concerts with her husband, who was a violinist. She noted in her diary about her visit to Kew, 'Wonderful concert. Men thrilled and thrilling.' Although the mess was 'not pleasant' there was 'lovely ice-cream'.

Paintings by Italian POWs remained on the windows of the Ruskin Avenue offices until they were demolished to make way for the Public Record Office. (Photo Pat Thomas)

Others were less welcoming. Some wrote outraged letters to the local newspaper complaining that enemy prisoners were being treated like 'guests and tourists' by the Vicar. (Evan Hopkins replied that it was simply an act of Christian charity.) The underlying difficulty was that they were in the middle of the suburbs of a city. Most prisoner of war camps were in the countryside away from towns as the prisoners worked on the land. 'A most unsuitable place to have a POW camp,' the local Police Superintendent wrote, adding, 'No local residents exactly welcome having such a camp in their locality.'

The second problem was the lack of recreational facilities: the Italian prisoners were allowed out of their camp after their work between 7 and 10 in the evening. Not all two thousand left every evening; many did, as there was little to keep them in Ruskin Avenue. There was a band, *I Sette Nani* (the Seven Dwarfs) and many cultivated hobbies, but there was no organised recreation or facilities for recreation on site, as there were for the Americans. Unlike the Americans too, they were not allowed into pubs or onto public transport. So most of them congregated on Kew

Green and Kew Bridge, 'to beguile themselves,' as the police said, 'by watching the river traffic or any games on the Green'. To many Kew residents they seemed a strange and scruffy horde; to the Italians it must have been simply the normal *passegiata*, the evening promenade when everybody wanders up and down the main street and principal square of the town. Normal that is, except for one important difference: no girls.

Italian POWs with Mr Thomas on Kew Towpath (Photo Pat Thomas)

It was the Italian attitude to women that caused the greatest problem: they liked them; they wanted to get to know them. Many of these young men had been prisoners of war for years and had therefore been deprived of female company. As co-operators, unlike normal prisoners of war, they were allowed to talk to any member of the public and accept invitations to visit private houses, but 'any relationship, or attempt to establish relations with women of a sexual or amorous character' was prohibited. (The character, we assume, was that of the relations, not the women.) It was just such a relationship that many of the Italians wanted. In contrast to the Americans, the Italians had very little money; they were ill-dressed; they were not glamorous; they did not speak English: so they had to rely on charm – charm or cheek. They pointed, for example, to the title ITALY on the shoulder of their uniform and explained it stood for 'I Trust And Love You'. Some attempts to make contact were distinctly touching. Moira Grinberg, who lived in Defoe Avenue at this time, recalls that she had an allotment plot between the towpath and the camp. 'My tool box leaned against the fencing. We were told not to communicate with the Italian prisoners of war – not easy as many of us saw them as fellow human beings, imprisoned. They tried talking to me while I worked, until they were herded in by a guard. One morning it was quiet in their compound. I opened my box and found a small heap of crumpled papers; love letters in broken English, drawings of me and my flowers.'

The charm was not always appreciated. Different cultures, different customs, mutual misunderstandings, the liberty from the rules of home on the one hand, an underlying suspicious hostility and fear on the other, caused a sense of panic in some quarters in Kew. 'It is not safe for any decent woman to be on the highway after dark for fear of molestation in some form or other from these men,' wrote a complainant to the War Office in October 1945. 'For instance, yesterday evening a lady, while proceeding from Kew Gardens Railway Station to Maze Road, was accosted by eight of these Italians, who attempted to get into conversation with her. You must agree that this is a terrifying experience. Furthermore I have information that this kind of behaviour is indulged in by these men throughout the immediate neighbourhood. In many cases their general conduct is both beastly and degrading to the extreme.'

In May the next year the Chairman of the Executive Committee of the Joint Committee of All Ratepayers Associations of Richmond wrote to the Police saying that they had had many complaints of the disgusting behaviour of the Italian POWs, of molestation of women and girls. He enquired, 'What is being done to control these uninvited and extremely ill-behaved men?' The Richmond Police investigated and found that there had been no specific complaints. The Superintendent concluded, 'I am quite satisfied that to say that women and girls are molested is a gross exaggeration. Some prisoners do smile at women when they receive encouragement...' – and here there is a new perspective, for he continued – 'and there is no doubt that women do "run after" these prisoners.' He added, 'The girls, who are more than willing parties, come from all parts of London to meet and associate with them.'

Italian officers, with Col Hobby, the British officer in charge of the Ruskin Avenue camp (Photo courtesy the Imperial War Museum)

The question is, 'Who was chasing whom?' Whatever it may have seemed to the Italians, it was men, not girls, who were scarce during war-time. Col. Hobby, the Camp Commandant, received 'numerous letters from girls in the neighbourhood addressed to various Italians, and also he received a few himself asking him not to punish them when they have been reported by the Civil Police for associating with the women'. Another police report said, 'On 11 May 1946 an Italian Corporal was found embracing a woman from Ilford at Richmond Towpath. She was a willing party; the Corporal has been reported.' Police were particularly worried about young girls below the age of consent – 16 girls under the age of 16 were dealt with for fraternising with Italians during June 1946. It was, however, the inevitable competition for a scarce resource that was going to cause the greatest trouble. British men, young civilians, but above all, servicemen, were angered by the sight of British girls associating with those they saw as the enemy – and what was clearly competition. The wrath, and the anxiety, of four sailors from the Kew area

(J. McQueen and A. McClaren, both of Sandycombe Road, R. Maskell of Bicester Road and J. Poland of Chaucer Avenue) on board HMS *Wolfe*, a navy depot ship, in the far east, exploded in a letter to the *Richmond Herald* when they heard of the Vicar's plan for a club for the Italians. Having expressed their 'smouldering contempt' for the Italians, they turned on a different target.

'Perhaps the worthy young women of Richmond whose main interests have been in a spacious building at the bottom of Ruskin Avenue since December, 1941, will find this club a new centre of interest and attraction, enhanced by a completely new array of foreign uniforms. Indeed, throughout the war Richmond girls have given their own countrymen the cold shoulder; if a man wore a uniform which was not British, he was the "cat's whiskers" to them. Is fraternisation going to be carried to the extent where our infatuated local girls may throw themselves en mass at our late enemies? Are any steps to be taken to prevent such an occurrence?' They concluded by suggesting, 'The money for a club could be better employed in equipping these prisoners of war with picks, shovels, etc. to repair the damage wrought upon our town by their Fascist partners in aggression,' which was, of course, precisely what the Italians were doing.

The simmering hostility flared up in mid-summer 1945 into a series of incidents that were going to worry not merely the local Police and Camp authorities, but also the Government and the military. It was perhaps inevitable that the spark occurred near the Boathouse. The band and the dancing attracted a large 'casual and floating population' from all around, including many British servicemen. The Italians were not allowed in but many wandered every evening up from the Green to Kew Bridge and near the pub, often to see if they could get into conversation with any female company.

Corporal Pietro Liparotti's version of events was that some time after 8'clock on Thursday 28 June, he was walking with his friend Private Giuseppe Giunti near the steps by the Boathouse when he met two sailors, some soldiers and civilians, all about 18 to 20 years old. A sailor asks the obvious question, 'Any women down this road?' to which he replies, 'I see no women down this road.' Then, observing the strict logic of such events, the sailor pulls up his sleeves and challenges, 'Come on, fight.' Liparotti demurs, 'I not fight. I no give trouble, you not give me trouble.' The sailor dismisses him, 'Get away, you f.....' Saying, 'O.K.', the Italians turn to leave, but a civilian insists, 'Come on, fight.' Despite Liparotti's protest, 'Me no fight. Me go camp,' the fight begins.

The British version of events, however, was different. One Italian with a group of six to eight friends was talking to a young lady outside the Boathouse. She wanted nothing to do with them, as she was waiting for a sailor. When he arrived, he got into an argument with the Italian and ended by punching him. The Italians attacked the sailor and a general fight ensued.

Whoever started it, the fight sucked in a number of men on both sides. It moved up and down the steps to the bridge and up and down the towpath. Various people tried to stop the fight. Mrs Annie Louisa Bavin, of no.1 York Villas, next to the towpath down from the bridge looked out of her bedroom window where she saw five youths and a British soldier fighting with an Italian. The Italian was not defending himself. Mrs Bavin shouted at the youths and said 'Here stop that, I'll phone the Police.' One of the youths then said to her, 'You side with the Italians.' She replied, 'Not at all, but it's not fair for all of you to be on him.' The youth made the damning accusation, 'That Italian has been talking to my sister.' The youths then moved off to the nearby tennis court.

The British said they were outnumbered by the Italians; the Italians that they were outnumbered by the British. Certainly sticks were used, certainly the British went into the Boathouse and armed themselves with glasses and bottles. Were the Italians all using knives? They denied it, but certainly someone on each side used a knife, because the end result was that one Italian and one British soldier ended up in hospital with knife wounds. Pte Leslie Eric Friday, who had four wounds in his back, which in fact were only superficial, was rushed in a passing American jeep to Brentford Cottage hospital; Giuseppe Giunti had a stab wound in his chest and was taken to Kingston Emergency Hospital.

The police were not particularly worried about this 'minor fracas' that was all over in a short time. Three days later on Sunday 1 July 1945, however, the situation threatened to get more serious. Again there was a fight outside the Boathouse about 9 o'clock in the evening. Mrs Kane, the licensee, called the police, nine of whom arrived to find the situation quiet with about 50 Italian co-operators standing in small groups on Kew Bridge and civilians waiting on the footways expectantly. The police decided to clear the area and the people dispersed quietly. The Captain Interpreter attached to the Camp said the Italian version was that the trouble started because a sailor and a gang of youths discharged a firework, presumed by the Italians to have been a pistol.

The police account continues. 'Five or six minutes later a body of Italians number 150-200, some armed with sticks and pieces of iron and adopting a threatening attitude, were seen approaching Kew Bridge from the Camp, ostensibly bent on following and attacking a gang of youths, who had gone across Kew Bridge to the Brentford side.'

The Police formed a cordon and stopped the Italians. Despite requests from Police, and a few unarmed guards and Italian pickets wearing yellow armbands, for the mob to return to Camp, they remained hostile and a 12 inch by ¾ inch iron bolt was thrown.

Police were forced to draw truncheons and marshalled them away from the British and back to Camp where they were 'ordered to their huts'. What caused these incidents? The Sub-divisional Inspector of Richmond Police was clear, 'There is little doubt that the presence of these Italians is not welcome, but the root cause of this particular disturbance is a gang of youths who, it is believed, come from Brentford for the sole purpose of causing trouble.' (The reference was to the 15-year-old Billy Angel and his friends.) The Superintendent explained, 'It appears that certain people of the rough element come over from Brentford and Chiswick and if they find these Italian Prisoners talking to or fraternising with English women, as is frequently the case, they take umbrage, pass hostile remarks and this of course leads to trouble.'

What worried the authorities, however, was how quickly so large a group could band together and arm themselves. (Apart from the sticks and pieces of iron, one policeman saw a number of the Italians drawing knives.) An armed mob of several hundred prisoners of war going on the rampage would surely lead to pitched battles and worse. The camp Commandant put Kew Green and parts of the Towpath out of bounds to the Italians. They were forbidden to assemble in groups of more than three and civilian and military patrols were instituted.

Apart from these disturbances, there seem to have been no major cases of friction between the Italians and the British, although one prisoner was assaulted on the Lower Mortlake Road and found with a strap round his neck. Camp life appears to have proceeded equably, but one prisoner, 34-year-old, Carlo Trincia, committed suicide. Another escaped; as the full police description was, 'He is 29, has brown hair, and may have a beard', one wonders if they ever found him.

One question did, however, concern, upset and anger the Italians: when were they going home? The war ended in Europe in May 1945 and then in August in Japan. With the shortage of shipping, they obviously could not all go at once, but the British government appeared to be making no plans. And indeed they were not. It had been proposed to Churchill, as Prime Minister, in June that Italian prisoners of war should be repatriated; his reply was a scathing refusal to consider it. Later, the farmers and the Ministry of Agriculture insisted that Italian labour was necessary for the potato and beet harvest. So it was only in December that the first groups of prisoners began to be repatriated. Month by month more of the 150,000 Italian prisoners of war were sent back to Italy. On 2 March 1946 the weekly club run by the parish church in Kew, 'the Italian Prisoners' Canteen', held their last meeting; the Italians presented an oil painting of an Italian harvest field, painted by one of the men, as a gift to the Church Hall. With the exception of a working party of 20, all the Italians had gone by 2 July 1946, some seventeen months after they had first arrived.

All were repatriated; although a thousand or so who were working on farms in other parts of the country were permitted to remain, none from Kew were allowed to stay. This would have unfortunate results for individuals. Relationships were broken. An unhappily married woman in Whitton had struck up a friendship with an Italian from Kew. He had given her two pairs of the co-operators' green battledress trousers, a fine gift in days of war-time clothes coupons, which she hoped to make into slacks, and a quantity of tools, presumably to sell. Her husband had found the stolen goods; he reported her to the police; he left her; he took their three young children to his sister. Then she found she was pregnant. A soldier returned home to Mortlake after several years' service abroad to discover his wife had had a baby; and the father was an Italian from Kew, by now back in Italy. He threatened to throw the baby off the balcony of their block of flats and was only persuaded not to do so by his own children.

Other cases were much happier. Luciano Demattia had had the job of collecting stores from the NAAFI depot in Brentford, and had met Vera Picton, who was working there. He courted her, but, like all the other Italians, was forced to return to Italy. He, however, managed to return after the war; they got married and he lived until his death in Brentford, working as an engineer on typewriters. He died in 1983 and is survived by his wife and daughter, Angela.

The Government intended to use the camp for German prisoners of war. It was redesignated No.144 Germany PW Working Camp, and immediately after the Italians left at the start of July 1946 a working party of 20 German prisoners arrived. Their job was to make it more secure and to construct it so that prisoners, who would not be allowed out after work, would have no access to the general public. The idea was that after a month or so 2000 German prisoners would come, but the plan was abandoned.

The Military finally vacated the premises on 20 September 1946, and returned it to civilian use. The Post Office already occupied some of the buildings at the camp and the Post Office Savings Bank's accounts and ledgers department was soon brought there. The smaller Unemployment Record Office, which was now in the Ministry of National Insurance, returned. These two institutions were to remain for the life of the buildings; other government, local government and Post Office departments used bits of the site at various times. Did they find traces of the American or Italian presence? Residents remember a guard tower being there for many years and paintings that the Italians had made remained, some until the buildings were demolished.

The demolition began in 1972 (the eastern part where the Inland Revenue Sorting Office was remained.) The following year work began on the new Public Record Office building, the Brutalist construction popularly known as Fort Ruskin. The work took four years and in October 1977 the new PRO building was opened to the public. In 1995 the new extension was opened and in 2003 the PRO was rebranded as The National Archives.

CHAPTER 7 – *THE AFTERMATH*

Everyone who lived through the war has special memories of the wild scenes of enthusiasm that greeted the end of the war in Europe on VE Day. (VJ Day, which marked the end of war with Japan a few months later, was generally celebrated more soberly, perhaps because of concern over the use of the atomic bomb.) Pat Thomas summed up the reaction of a teenager in Kew: 'VE Day was the happiest day of my life. There was a big bonfire on the green and we burnt an effigy of Hitler. We were ecstatic with joy.'

Victory Celebrations in Bushwood Road (Photo Pat Thomas)

War and the threat of war had dominated life in Britain for more than five years. It was time to celebrate. Street parties were organised all over Kew. Many photographs survive of those parties. They happily record who were there to cheer, but they also act as a reminder of how very few pictures remain of the previous years in wartime Kew. The GIs took, and have preserved, a remarkable record of their days in Kew Barracks, but the British civilians were starved of film, and we are heavily dependent on memories and the written word.

Fortunately, written records do survive. We have those of the ARP who listed the bombs that fell. We have lists of the civilian dead, and of the houses that were rebuilt. (These lists are on pages 66-71.) These official records are invaluable. They give a vivid picture of the damage to life and property, but they do not give the whole picture. They were mostly compiled in very difficult circumstances, and often in a hurry; inevitably there are omissions and inconsistencies. Here, as elsewhere, we should appreciate further information from those who have it, so that we can do more to bring the records up to date in future editions of this book.

There are still a few – surprisingly few, in view of the shocking damage to wartime Kew – mementos of the war that can still be glimpsed around the streets and along the riverside. On Kew Bridge itself, on the plaque that reminds us of its proper name ('The King Edward VII Bridge') there are scars made by the bomb that fell on the bridge in February 1944. There are scars too on the opposite parapet. This bomb fell in the raid that Ron Draper describes so dramatically on page 14. There was a block house at the foot of the bridge then; it is long gone, but one block house does survive. It is by the railway. Look out of the train to your left, as your travel to London. It is just short of the railway bridge. It is now covered by a mass of creepers, but generations of children have played there – presumably quite illegally, as it is on railway property.

The Pill Box on the embankment, seen from the Forest Road houses, backed by a District Line train (Photo Pat Thomas)

At the foot of High Park Avenue, beneath the bridge, and now concealed behind the bushes, there is a locked door. It was, Roy Featherstone recalls, a wardens' post, while opposite on the roof of 96 North Rd, then the police station, was the siren that screamed out its air-raid warning day after day and night after night in 1940-1 and again in 1944-45.

There are reminders too of how traffic struggled in the war. Just one or two of the trees along the Kew Road retain marks of the two bands of white paint – now rapidly fading like the memories of those who lived through the war – that made it possible to negotiate the road in the darkness of the blackout. The two trees mostly clearly marked are close the bus stops by the Avenue and Lion Gate.

Remarkably, one of the biggest air-raid shelters in the whole village is still in perfect condition. It was built by the authorities beneath the lawn of Leyborne Lodge. Michael Atwood, the last of his family to live there, remembers that it was built to accommodate up to fifty of the refugees that had settled in Kew. It was fitted with a chemical loo and a kitchenette. The McGraths, who now own the house, annually encourage children from the Queen's School to explore it and experience what it must have been like to take refuge underground from the Blitz.

Almost all of the smaller shelters have been dismantled, or filled in. It is easy to speculate where some of them might have stood – Kew has an exceptional number of rockeries! However, we do know of at least one Anderson shelter that has been kept and used as an apple store – most appropriately as it is situated where orchards flourished in the 19th century. There must be others, all them now buildings of historic, if not architectural, interest. If you know of a survivor do please let us know.

There are other legacies of the war that are less characteristic of wartime architecture than Anderson shelters and block houses, but they may outlast them. These are the houses that were built on the sites of those that were bombed. Many of them were designed to match the houses they replaced; others were distinctly different. Most of them are listed in pages 66-71. The list does not, however, include the eight houses that replace those destroyed by the V2 that fell behind West Park Avenue in 1944. By chance, one of them is now the home of Joan Rundle, whose grandfather, Ernest Ridge, died in that attack. She points out that the rebuilt houses differ from their neighbours in that they lack cellars, and that it is probable that their original cellars were filled with rubble from the bombing. Mrs Fortune, who had bought one of these houses in 1936 for £900, came back to live in the rebuilt house in Nov 1949. 'The government had allowed £2700 for rebuilding,' she recalled, 'but it was not enough.' The Fortunes had to add money of their own.

Unexpectedly, the least helpful of the records that remain of the war are the records of those who went off to fight, and of those who died in battle. We are all familiar with the war memorials set up in every town and village at the end of the First World War, and the sobering sight of the long lists of those fallen in battle. Many authorities used the same memorials for those who fell in the Second World War, placing their names below or on the reverse side of the memorial. Not so in Richmond. The memorial below the old Town Hall in Whittaker Avenue covers those in the old borough of Richmond who died in the forces – and therefore should include all of those from Kew – but it lists only those who died in the First World War. The Borough does however include the Second World War names in a book of remembrance, kept in the old Town Hall. For most of the fallen of the First World War – but for very few from the Second World War – there are supplementary details on where the death occurred and even the home address.

In Kew itself we have a number of memorials that do not contain names and two that do. Among the former are the War Memorial gardens at Westerly Ware, the cross on Kew Green, and a wooden plaque in the Barn Church. However, St Anne's does have the names of those parishioners who died in both World Wars on an oak screen, and the Royal Botanic Gardens has a brass plaque that displays the names of student gardeners and administrators, both past and present, known to have been killed in the war.

Written records are equally sparse. Parish magazines of the war years included scarcely any references to war deaths, and the local press was hardly more helpful, with one famous exception. The Richmond local papers regularly printed the weekly score of the local Spitfire ace, Brendan 'Paddy' Finucane, with almost gladiatorial glee. The Finucane family lived in Castlegate, from 1936 to 1938; they attended St Winefride's church in Leyborne Park, and Paddy went to Cardinal Vaughan School. Paddy was the superstar of his time. The Allies youngest ever Wing Commander, he died before he reached the age of 22. He is commemorated locally in a very special way, giving his name to a block a flats: Finucane Court lies just on the corner of Kew, in Stanmore Gardens, a few yards from where he lived as a teenager.

Sadly, there seems to be no listing anywhere of those who fought and then came home. Then, as now, the nation has found no way to express appropriate thanks for their commitment to the country's defence. Those of us whose parents fought in the war know how little they liked to talk of their experiences. Few wrote of them. So their names are treasured only in the memory of the families who welcomed them back home.

APPENDIX – *TABLES: BOMBS*

TABLE 1		WHERE THE BOMBS FELL *(from Borough of Richmond Bomb Report)*	
DATE	*TIME*	*INCIDENT*	*TYPE OF BOMB*
1940			
16th September	03.55	Gordon Road	H.E.
	03.55	Victoria Road [Cottages]	H.E.
	03.55	29/31 The Avenue	H.E.
	03.55	13 Lawn Crescent	H.E.
	03.55	5/7 Ennerdale Road	H.E.
	03.55	12 Lichfield Road	H.E.
	03.55	25 Alexandra Road	H.E.
	03.55	10 Clarence Road	H.E.
24th September	00.05	21 West Park Road	H.E.
	00.20	70 Mortlake Road	H.E.
	03.55	Defoe Avenue	H.E.
	04.00	Kew Gardens	H.E.
	04.00	Kew Green	Incendiary
	04.00	24 Beechwood Avenue	H.E.
	04.00	Fair Ground, Kew Bridge	H.E.
	04.00	250/252 Kew Road	Incendiary
	05.25	6 Westhall Road	H.E.
26th September	03.00	139 Sandycombe Road	Mine
29th September	00.20	South Ave. Sandycombe Road	Incendiary
	00.20	Sewerage Farm	H.E.
	00.20	Victoria Road [Cottages]	H.E.
	01.35	45 Chilton Road	Incendiary
30th September	21.55	28/29 West Park Road	H.E.
	21.55	129 Mortlake Road	Oil Bomb
	21.55	Chrysler Motors Roadway	H.E.
	21.55	Ministry of Labour, Kew	H.E.
	21.55	Fulham Cemetery	Mine
	21.55	West Park Road	H.E.
1st October	02.40	St. Paul's Church, Raleigh Rd.	H.E.
	02.40	South Ave., Sandycombe Road	Incendiary
4th October	00.20	Corner High Park Avenue Pensford Avenue	Incendiary

TABLE 1 (contd. - 2)	WHERE THE BOMBS FELL		
DATE 1940	*TIME*	*INCIDENT*	*TYPE OF BOMB*
4th October	00.21	Chelwood Gardens passage connecting Pensford Avenue	Oil Bomb
	00.25	284 Kew Road junction Kew Gardens Road	H.E.
	00.48	Beechwood Avenue	H.E.
7th October	21.21	Mortlake Road	Incendiary
		Beechwood Avenue	Incendiary
		Burlington Avenue	Incendiary
		Nylands Avenue	Incendiary
		Atwood Avenue	Incendiary
		High Park Road	Incendiary
	21.28	17 Nylands Avenue	Incendiary
	21.30	30 The Avenue	Incendiary
	21.35	Mortlake Road	Incendiary
		West Park Avenue	Incendiary
		Defoe Avenue	Incendiary
		Ruskin Avenue	Incendiary
13th October	21.30	Chrysler Motors	H.E. H.E/UXB
15th October	22.20	Kew Gardens	2 H.E.
19th October	19.25	Niton Road	H.E.
	19.25	Darell Road School	Oil Bomb
	19.25	10/11 North Road	H.E.
	20.12	196 Kew Road	Incendiary
		34 Ennerdale Road	Incendiary
		Clareville, Lion Gate Gardens	Incendiary
28th October	04.30	Junction Hatherley Road and Kew Road	H.E.
	04.30	Kew Gardens near Palm House	H.E.
8th November	21.10	Chrysler Works grounds	H.E.
	21.10	Fulham Cemetery	H.E./UXB
	21.10	288 Sandycombe Road	H.E.
	21.10	Sewerage Works	H.E.
	21.10	17 Beechwood Avenue	H.E.
	00.25	Junction High Park Avenue and Pensford Avenue	H.E.
	002.5	50 Pensford Avenue	H.E.

TABLE 1 (contd. - 3)		WHERE THE BOMBS FELL	
DATE 1940	**TIME**	**INCIDENT**	**TYPE OF BOMB**
12th November	19.20	Clarence Road	H.E.
	19.20	Kew Road, nr. Lichfield Road	H.E.
	19.20	4 Clarence Road in roadway	H.E./UXB
	19.20	Fulham Cemetery	H.E.
	19.20	Kew gardens (Richmond side Palm House in Pagoda Vista)	H.E.
	20.20	Military Post Ministry of Labour	H.E.
	20.23	15 yds North Towpath opposite Strand on Green Island	H.E.
	20.23	Towing path front of Sewerage Works	H.E.
16th November	23.55	17 Gloucester Road	Incendiary
	23.55	24 Forest Road	Incendiary
	23.55	5,13,29 Maze Road	Incendiary
	23.55	65 Gloucester Road and Cumberland Works	Incendiary
	23.55	29 Mortlake Road	Incendiary
	23.55	42,44,68,81 Beechwood Road	Incendiary
	23.55	8 Priory Road	Incendiary
	23.55	14, 18 Priory Road	Incendiary
	23.55	21 Haverfield Gardens	Incendiary
	23.55	Ministry of Labour	Incendiary
	23.55	Grampion Works, Station Parade	Incendiary
	23.55	8 Ennerdale Road	Incendiary
	23.55	44 Beechwood Avenue	Incendiary
	23.55	Fulham Cemetery, Thompson Avenue	Incendiary
	01.45	Back of Nylands Avenue	H.E.
	02.12	Kew Gardens, west side of Broad Walk	H.E.
20th November	03.30	5 West Park Road	Incendiary
	03.30	207 Mortlake Road	Incendiary
	03.30	Taylor Avenue	Incendiary
29th November	19.33	15 Thompson Avenue	Incendiary
	19.33	17 Popham Gardens	Incendiary
	19.33	8,12,13,18 Popham Gardens	Incendiary

TABLE 1 (contd. - 4)	WHERE THE BOMBS FELL		
DATE **1940**	*TIME*	*INCIDENT*	*TYPE OF BOMB*
29th November	20.15	13 Markesbury Avenue	Incendiary
	20.15	Richmond Main Sewerage Wks	H.E./UXB
	20.15	Mortlake Road	H.E./UXB
	22.50	Opposite 15 Atwood Avenue	H.E.
	23.10	10 Taylor Avenue, 1 High Park Gardens	H.E.
1st December	00.00	Nth. Sheen Recreation Ground	H.E.
1941			
8th March	21.15	6 Kew Meadow Path	H.E.
	21.15	Kew Meadow Path	4 H.E.
	21.10	Lodge Gate, Hammersmith Cemetery	H.E. Incendiary
	21.10	Fulham Cemetery	H.E.
	21.10	Kew Gardens	2 H.E.
1944			
19th February		Watkinsons Field	50 Kilo Phosphorus
		Mortlake Road	50 Kilo Pho
24th February		Kew Gardens	H.E./UXB 2 HE 4Phos/UXB
26th June	15.30	Watkins Field	Fly Bomb
27th August	06.50	Records Office, Kew	Fly Bomb
12th September	06.15	Chryslers, Kew	V.2. L.R.R.

APPENDIX – *TABLES: BOMBS*

TABLE 2		BOMBED SITES Number of Houses Destroyed	
	Road	*House nos.*	*Number of houses destroyed*
	(from Borough of Richmond *Bomb Report)*		
1.	**Alexandra Road**	23-27	3
2.	**Beechwood Avenue**	18-24 37-43	8
3.	**Clarence Road**	8-11	4
4.	**Defoe Avenue**	50-54	3
5.	**Kew Road**	284, 286 224	3
6.	**Marksbury Avenue**	33,35	2
7.	**Niton Road**	22-28	4
8.	**Raleigh Road**	2 19-25	5
9.	**Sandycombe Road**	288,290 272	3
	(not included in Borough of Richmond *Bomb Report)*		
10.	**West Park Avenue**	34-48	8
	Total number of houses destroyed in Kew		*43*

APPENDIX – *Victims of the Bombs in Kew*

Twenty-nine people died in Kew as a result of bombing during the Second World War: the oldest was 71; the youngest were 2 years old. 19 were killed during the Blitz of late 1940 and 10 during the "Second Blitz", the flying bomb and rocket attacks of 1944 and early 1945.

The worst night in Kew was 25th September 1940 when 14 people were killed in the **Beechwood Avenue** area, including **Camiel Dangez** (aged 57) and his son **Herman** (14), who were refugees who had escaped from Belgium. At no. 22 Beechwood Avenue **William Preston** (58), his wife **Elizabeth** (63) and his son **Barratt** (32) were killed as well as **Mildred O'Malley** (56) and **Sarah Hart** (39). Next door at no. 24 **Isabella Robinson** and her daughter **Coral** (30) were victims. These and two other neighbouring houses were destroyed – the new houses rebuilt after the war are easy to spot. Similarly, further up the road on the other side, another four houses were destroyed, including no. 39, where **Francis** (62) and **Gertrude** (61) **Stebbing** died. At the corner of Beechwood Avenue and West Park Road at no. 13 West Park Road **William Shaw** (41), his wife **Frances** (33) and **Harriet Fletcher** (65) were in the shelter, but that did not save them.

Nearly a month later on 19th October a bomb hit 11 **North Road**, killing the **Charkin** family, **Cyril** (30), **Josephine** (27) and their baby son **Michael** (2), as well as **William Cushin** (71). Another two-year-old, **Robert Hawtin**, died on 7th November when 288 **Sandycombe Road** (next to the Kew Gardens Hotel) was bombed.

After the Blitz there was very little bombing until the summer of 1944. On 27th August 1944 a V1 flying bomb (doodlebug) hit the **Ruskin Avenue** offices (now the site of the National Archives) which were being used as barracks by the US Army; three Americans died, including **Lt. John Calley** and **Sgt. Jack Portrum**.

On 12th September a V2 rocket struck the **Chrysler Motor Works** (now Kew Retail Park), killing **Ernest Ridge** (51) of Bushwood Road who was on fire duty, as well as **Cecil Atkinson** (45**), Ernest Payze** (33), **Gilbert Saville** (33) and **James Richardson** (28), all four from Twickenham, with **Henry McDonald** (36) from Southall, and **Robert Ritson** (50), who had come all the way from Gateshead.